PATCHWORK

TRADITIONAL NEEDLE ARTS

PATCHWORK

25 classic step-by-step projects

DIANA LODGE

PHOTOGRAPHY BY JAN BALDWIN

THUNDER BAY
P·R·E·S·S

To Roy, without whose artistic skills, together with his moral and practical support, this book would never have been written.

Published by
Thunder Bay Press
5880 Oberlin Drive, Suite 400
San Diego, California 92121

First published in Great Britain in 1994 by
Mitchell Beazley
an imprint of Reed Consumer Books Limited
Michelin House, 81 Fulham Road, London SW3 6RB
and Auckland, Melbourne, Singapore and Toronto

Art Director	JACQUI SMALL
Executive Editor	JUDITH MORE
Executive Art Editor	LARRAINE SHAMWANA
Editors	CATHERINE WARD, ELIZABETH RADFORD, HEATHER DEWHURST
Production	ALISON MYER
Design	MAGGIE TOWN & BOBBY BIRCHALL
Illustrations	KEVIN HART

Library of Congress Cataloging-in-Publication data

Lodge, Diana
    Patchwork: 25 classic step-by-step projects/
  Diana Lodge; photography by Jan Baldwin.
  p. cm. - (Traditional needle arts)
Includes index.
ISBN 1 57145 010 6
1. Patchwork - Patterns. 2. Quilting - Patterns.
I. Title. II. Series.
TT835.162 1994   94-16516
746.46 - dc20   CIP

The publishers have made every effort to ensure that all instructions given in this book are accurate and safe but they cannot accept liability for any resulting injury, damage or loss to either person or property, whether direct or consequential and howsoever arising.
The author and publishers will be grateful for any information which will assist them in keeping future editions up to date.

Typeset in Perpetua 12.5/16pt 11.5/16pt and 11.5/12pt
Index compiled by James Partiger
Printed and bound in Great Britain
by Butler & Tanner Ltd.

Contents

Introduction

Unique among antiques, quilts have a tactile humanity that is like a direct contact with the past. Perhaps only a piece of jewelry, handed down through the years, has the same capacity for putting us in touch with earlier generations. The patchwork quilts chosen for this book were made between the middle of the 19th century and the 1930s, and represent a geographical spread from Europe to the United States. They have been chosen to offer a variety of types and patterns, including American block patterns and Log Cabin designs, medallions, traditional English-style patchwork made with backing papers, and several made in the northeast of England and embellished with quilting designs.

No single race, area, or class can claim to have discovered patchwork; its origins are as diverse as those of the women who made the quilts in this book. A whole range of traditions and skills are combined in the great creative flowering of patchwork patterns and designs that took place in America toward the latter half of the 19th century. From the earliest days, women have pieced together lengths of fabric when there was not enough of a single cloth for their purpose, but patchwork as an intentional design form did not really exist until some time after the first English colonists had arrived in the New World.

In the 16th and 17th centuries, quilted clothing was high fashion throughout Europe, and production was in the hands of professionals, mainly men. Quilts had existed even in the Middle Ages, and a will of 1477 refers to "unum twylt," among other bedding. However, quilted covers were rare and found only in noble households; they were also wholecloth, not patchwork.

Patchwork, as we think of it, really began when the English East India Company (granted a royal charter in 1600) began to bring home cargoes of colorfast Indian muslin and chintz,

TOP AND ABOVE Red and white was the most popular of all color combinations for patchwork quilts, but if you don't want to keep to these colors, experiment with other colors on graph paper, drawing the quilt to scale; or you can make up a block in your chosen fabric by cutting pieces to the finished size and gluing them to paper.

TOP AND ABOVE Even simple patchwork designs, such as that in the top picture, in which rows are set diagonally and colors mixed at random, or above, where patches are joined in strips, can be highly effective when the colors harmonize.

beautifully decorated with prints of exotic birds and flowers. These lovely fabrics were highly sought for clothing, furnishings, and for quilts. Indian fabrics were expensive, however, and even scraps were hoarded and pieced together carefully. The earliest surviving patchwork quilt of this nature is the Levens Hall quilt. This was made from muslin in 1708 by members of the family, who then owned the hall, near Kendal in the North of England.

The patchwork of the Levens Hall quilt is of the mosaic style, in which small repeated shapes are pieced together in an overall pattern. Also popular at this time were medallion quilts, in which an interesting central piece was surrounded by a series of pieced borders. In England, both these patchwork types remained popular well into the Victorian era, especially the intricately pieced mosaic patchworks; mosaic patchwork, made with backing papers, is often known as English patchwork. This type of needlework was very much a reserve of the wealthy; only they could spare the time and fabric required. A typical example is the 19th-century mosaic quilt made from silk ballgowns which lies on an Elizabethan bed in the fairytale castle at Dunster, home of the Luttrell family since the Middle Ages. In humbler English homes, the most common form of patchwork quilt was a "strippy." This was made by joining lengths of fabric, sometimes with a pieced central strip, and then quilting the patchwork.

In America, patchwork initially developed along similar lines to England. Chintz was equally popular among the wealthy, and one of the earliest surviving American patchwork quilts, allegedly made by Martha Washington, is in the medallion style. By the early years of the 19th century, however, a style was emerging that was to become a uniquely American art form – the block pattern – in which the overall design was created by repeating smaller pieced squares. In the 18th century, quilting and embroidery skills were regarded as social accomplishments; however, by the middle of the 19th century, all respectable women were expected to make quilts for their families, and designing blocks and quilt patterns became a form of folk art.

Early block patterns were usually joined with a lattice of sashing strips or alternated with plain squares, but as block patterns became more elaborate and popular, it was realized that some blocks, such as the Log Cabin design, could create new, large-scale patterns, depending on how the blocks were joined.

The block patterns developed in the 19th and early 20th centuries are staggering in their diversity and inventiveness, and fascinating as a social record. Names for block patterns, such as Rocky Road to California or Barn Raising, may reflect the pioneer lifestyle; many names, such as King David's Crown or Crown and Thorns, show the religious convictions of their inventors. Other blocks were named after the women who devised them: such as Aunt Eliza's Star or Aunt Sukey's Choice.

A girl would make up to 12 or 13 patchwork quilt tops, starting perhaps with a simple four-patch design, and finishing with the pride of her collection: her bride's quilt. The pieced tops were kept in her hope chest, ready to be quilted once she was engaged. The final assembling of the layers and stitching of a quilt was a social event – the quilting bee – in which friends and neighbors would join, turning the sewing task into a party. Here, the American and English traditions remained similar; my godmother, Ann Taylor, remembers similar quilting/social gatherings from her childhood in the northeast of England.

Some of the quilts in this book are straightforward and may well have been made by young girls; others display more highly developed sewing skills. Some, such as the Iowa Amish Crown and Thorns, are beautifully conceived and executed; others, such as the Postage Stamp quilt, are charming but eccentric. In each case, the quilt provides an insight into the life and character of the maker – perhaps they contain scraps from the dresses she and her family wore; maybe well-worn fabrics have been lovingly preserved, as in the case of the Bordered Chain quilt.

Whichever pattern you choose, it will bear your stamp; hopefully, it will come to be treasured, not just for its beauty, but as a part of your own family history.

TOP A scrap-bag quilt can be given cohesion by restricting certain colors or pattern types to particular rows. BELOW Plain half-blocks are cleverly used to create the zigzag effect of this Canadian Star coverlet.

How to Begin

MATERIALS AND EQUIPMENT
Fabrics

The quilts featured in this book are nearly all made from dressweight pure cotton. This is easy to sew, frays relatively little, is hardwearing, and remains the ideal fabric to use for patchwork.

New fabrics may shrink and are not always colorfast, so before cutting out your fabrics, prewash them. Clip into the selvages to prevent uneven shrinkage, then put the fabrics through a hot machine wash (without detergent, but with a small amount of fabric conditioner). If you suspect that a fabric is not colorfast, soak it in a solution of three parts cold water to one part vinegar. Rinse thoroughly, and then wash again with a piece of white fabric. If the latter is discolored, discard the suspect fabric.

Most of the antique quilts in this book were made with a cotton filler, but polyester batting is more readily available and is inexpensive. If you choose the latter, you will find that the lighter, 2 oz, weight is the best for hand sewing. Thicker types give more "loft" (the relief effect characteristic of quilting), but are harder to stitch through.

NOTE

Unless otherwise stated, the fabric quantities listed with each project assume a standard fabric width of 45 in. If your fabric is wider or narrower than this, you will have to estimate the length required; you will find how to do this on page 102.

Equipment

Rotary cutter This is used for the multiple cutting of patchwork pieces and is ideal for cutting borders, bindings, and all straightforward pieces, such as squares, rectangles, and triangles. Replace the blade guard when the cutter is not in use.

Self-healing mat Available from art suppliers, this is required for use with a rotary cutter.

Rulers A quilter's ruler, which is a large, wide plastic ruler marked with angles and a grid, is essential for use with a rotary cutter, and in many cases avoids the need for templates and/or marking the fabric. A long ruler and a rolling ruler are also useful for marking quilting patterns.

Needles For hand sewing, use sharps 8 or 9. For machine stitching dressweight fabrics, use size 90 (14) needles.

Threads Ordinary dressmaking thread can be used for hand sewing, but pure cotton quilting thread is stronger. Use the same thread for quilting; you may find that it helps to strengthen the thread and assist it to pass smoothly through the layers if you run it through a beeswax block.

Use No.40 cotton or cotton/polyester thread for machine stitching cottons.

Pins Use either fine dressmakers' pins or fine brass lace pins. Long glass-headed pins are useful for pin-basting through layers.

Thimbles It is usual to wear a thimble on the middle finger of the (top) quilting hand when hand quilting.

Scissors Good-quality dressmaker's scissors are an essential tool for cutting out fabric; smaller embroidery scissors are useful for cutting thread ends.

Frames See page 14.

MARKING AND CUTTING FABRICS

The patches for several of the designs in this book can be cut with a rotary cutter and mat, without templates. For others, however, some or all of the pieces require templates. Patchwork templates may or may not include seam allowances, depending on the stitching method, and it is essential to make the appropriate template for your chosen method:

*For hand piecing, using running stitch, make templates to the exact geometric size, without seam allowances.

*For machine stitching, make templates with an additional ¼ in seam allowance all around. The line marked on the fabric is the cutting line.

*For the backing paper method (see page 13), you will require either two templates for each shape - one with seam allowances, for marking the fabric, and one without, for marking the papers — or, alternatively, a window template. This is made to the size of the unsewn fabric patch, with seam allowances, but with the central portion (the size of the stitched patch) removed. This has the advantage that you can use it to mark both papers and fabric patches, and can see to select a particular section of the fabric pattern for each shape.

*For quilting patterns to be marked with templates, cut to the shape of the outline, with or without long dashes to mark internal lines (see page 13).

Making templates
First either trace the template pattern or draw templates to scale on graph paper. None of the template patterns in this book includes a seam allowance, so add a ¼ in allowance around the marked outline, if appropriate for the intended sewing method (see above).

Leaving about ¾ in around each, cut out the template shapes; using spray adhesive, glue the shapes either to firm cardboard or to template plastic (available from quilting suppliers). Leave them to dry and then, using a craft knife, carefully cut out the shapes along the marked (outer) line.

Patchwork pieces with curved edges may have notches or circles to help when matching seam lines. Mark the seam line of the tracing, and then make a fine cut in the edge of the template when cutting it out.

If you are using cardboard for your templates and a shape is repeated frequently, make several to the same shape, as cardboard templates can become worn and inaccurate.

Marking the fabric
Lay the fabric right side down on a flat hard surface, and draw around the template with a sharp pencil. For hand piecing with a running stitch, leave a space of ½ in between each marked shape, and add a ¼ in seam allowance around each shape when cutting out. Templates for machine sewing or the backing paper method

include allowances, so butt the shapes up against each other, to avoid wastage.

When marking triangles, mark them with the longest edge running along the grainline whenever possible. Mark curved shapes with the curve on the bias, to allow them to be stretched and manipulated during sewing. To cut pairs of mirror-image patches, either, if cutting from a single layer, cut a patch and then flip the template over to cut the second (mirror-image) patch, or layer fabrics alternately wrong and right way up, for multiple cutting.

Patches can be cut with sharp dressmaking scissors or, more speedily, with a rotary cutter. If you are using scissors, you may cut patches one at a time, or you can layer up to four evenly-sized fabric pieces, matching grainlines. Mark the top layer only, and pin through the center of each marked shape, through all layers. In this way, it is possible to cut several patches at once.

With a rotary cutter, it is possible to cut through six to eight fabric layers, without pinning. Either layer several different fabrics together or, alternatively, fold and cut several patches at a time from a single length of fabric. To prepare fabric for cutting, fold it in half, matching selvages; steam press, and then fold in half again, taking the first foldline over to the selvages. Press again, and lay the folded fabric on a self-healing mat. Pressing down firmly on a quilter's ruler with one hand, trim away the folded (not selvage) edge of the fabric, by running the rotary cutter along the

edge of the ruler. Simple shapes can all be cut without templates, using the grid and angles marked on the ruler as a guide. For safety reasons, always push the blade away from you.

SEWING PATCHWORK
Running stitch method
Place two patches with right sides together, matching the marked

seam lines. Placing pins at right angles to the seam lines, pin first at the corners and then at intervals along the edge.

Thread a sharps needle with matching or neutral thread, knotting one end. Remove the corner pin at one end and insert the needle – do not sew through the seam allowances at either end of the patches. Sew along the

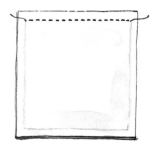

marked line with small, even running stitches, removing pins as you go. Finish with a double backstitch.

Machine stitching

Use the distance between the needle and the outer edge of the presser foot – usually a convenient ¼ in – to establish the width of the seam allowance, aligning the raw edge of the fabric with the edge of the foot. (If the space is not correct, put a strip of masking tape on the base plate at the

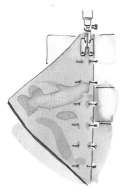

appropriate place.) Set your machine to 12 stitches per inch), and make a few back stitches at each end of the seam. For speed, you can batch-sew groups of identical patches without cutting the threads between pairs (but still back-stitching at the beginning and end of each individual seam line).

Joining patches

For inset patches, first join the pieces that form the angle,

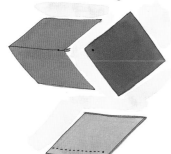

finishing ¼ in short of the stitching line.

Pin the piece to be inset along one side of the angle and, starting at the seam at the inner corner,

stitch from the inner angle to the outside edge.

Next, pin the inset piece to the facing side of the angle, as shown, and again stitch from the inner corner to the outside edge,

starting at the same point as the first stitching line.

Steam press the stitched pieces. Puckers at the corner can usually be eased out by removing a stitch from one of the seams.

In most cases, pieces are joined with raw edges aligning exactly, but where seams run at an angle – for example, when triangles are being joined into rectangles or diamonds, remember to join seam lines and not raw edges.

When joining rows and multiples of patches, pin carefully at each matching seamline, to ensure that the patches are correctly aligned.

When pinning border strips ready for stitching, mark and pin the border strips at measured intervals corresponding to the patchwork pattern, for an even fit. Even if a piece of patchwork has been handsewn, it is generally

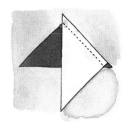

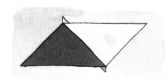

quicker and simpler to attach borders by machine stitching.

PRESSING

Press seams as you sew, and always before the next stage in the piecing sequence. Seams are normally pressed to one side, to reduce stress on the stitches, an exception being when a dense quilting design involves lines running across seams. Take the allowances to the darker side, to avoid them showing through. Press seam allowances on adjacent rows in opposite directions, to reduce bulk. When you have finished joining a block, and all the seams have been pressed, press the complete block on the right side, using a pressing cloth to avoid glazing the fabric.

BACKING PAPER METHOD

This hand-stitching technique is the most accurate method to use when piecing intricate shapes with angled seams. Two templates or a window template are required (see page 10). For the backing papers, use good-quality typing paper or paper of a similar thickness. Using the smaller, finished size of template, draw and cut a paper shape for each patch. For the fabric patches, use the larger template. When possible, make sure that the grain of the fabric runs in the same direction for each patch.

For the sewing method, refer to the Hexagon Star quilt on page 25. Use quilting thread in a matching or neutral color, knotting the end you have just cut (this will help to avoid tangles). Take care not to catch the papers as you stitch, and finish with a few reverse stitches.

QUILTING

A quilt is a sandwich of three layers – the top (in this book, patchwork), a middle layer of batting, and the back. On a purely practical level, the quilting stitches exist to hold these layers together, but they are also highly decorative, complementing the patchwork design and bringing it to life.

If the filling is cotton, as is the case with most of the old quilts in this book, the distance between quilting lines should not be larger than 2 in, but with modern polyester batting this can be increased to 3 in.

Making templates

These are made from either cardboard or template plastic, in the same way as patchwork templates (see page 11). You can either make outline templates, and then fill in any internal details by hand, or you can make stencil templates, cutting the major internal lines with long dashes, just wide enough to allow your pencil lead to pass through. Filling in the lines freehand has its advantages, however – it is not difficult, and the effect can be more natural and attractive than stenciled lines.

Marking your design

Mark your design on the finished patchwork top before assembling the layers (top, batting and backing) together. You will need a sharp H lead pencil (preferably a propelling pencil which will take a $\frac{1}{50}$ in lead), for light fabrics, and either a silver or soapstone pencil (available from specialist suppliers) for darker fabrics. Alternatively, you can use well-sharpened colored pencils, of a slightly darker shade than the fabric. You will also need a quilter's ruler for marking straight lines.

Very carefully, steam press the quilt top and lay it, right side up, on a large table. Use masking tape or tablecloth clips to anchor the fabric to the table and keep it taut. Keep your marking tools and templates on a side table, and make sure that you have access to all sides of the large table. First mark the outer edge of the quilting design with either a single or double line; bearing in mind the way in which the quilt edges will be finished – if the edges are

to be folded in, the quilting should stop 1 in clear of the raw edge, and in other cases it should stop about $\frac{1}{2}$ in clear. Next, draw motifs and border patterns; start at the centre of each border and work out to the corners, to ensure that the pattern is symmetrical.

Finally, draw any filling patterns, such as parallel lines or cross hatching. There is no need to draw lines for contour quilting, as these simply echo the lines of the patchwork seams. Check regularly with a ruler and set square or protractor as you are drawing filler patterns – it is all too easy to make mistakes here.

Using a hoop or tube frame

Once you have marked the quilt top, the next stage is to assemble the three layers – top, batting, and backing – together. If you are using a hoop or tube frame, mark the mid-point on each edge of each of the layers with pins, then carefully smooth out the well-pressed quilt back, wrong side up, on a large flat surface. Fold the batting in half and lay it on the back, matching marked mid-points. Gently unfold the batting over the second half of the back, again checking that pinned mid-points match. Fold the top into quarters, right side inside, and carefully place it over one quarter of the two prepared layers. Gradually unfold, matching up mid-points, and smoothing out wrinkles with a yardstick.

Pin the layers together, and then baste very thoroughly, as shown, with lines not more than 4 – 6 in apart. For basting lines running across the quilt, start at the center,

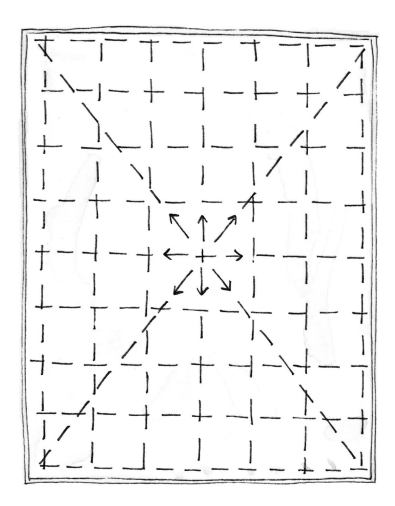

leaving a long tail and working out to one edge; rethread the needle at the center of the quilt and work out to the opposite edge. In this way, you will avoid a cluster of knots at the center.

Center the quilt over the inner hoop, carefully smoothing out the fabric; loosen the outer hoop and place it over the quilt and the inner hoop. Tighten the outer hoop, making sure that the layers are smooth at the back as well as the front and are evenly stretched. Start quilting at the center, radiating outward, and always remove the quilt after each

stitching session, to avoid marking the fabric.

Using a frame
Do not baste the layers together; instead, baste the backing fabric, wrong side up, to the webbing of the front and back rails and roll it up until flat; smooth the batting and then the top fabric over it, pinning and basting these to the near rail. At the far rail, pin the layers together and fold the excess batting and top fabrics, to prevent them from touching the floor. Use tape 1 in wide to tension the side edges, but leave enough flexibility

for stitching. Quilt across the top to the far rail; roll the completed section onto the near rail and finally re-pin and re-tape before continuing.

Quilting
Take an 18 in length of quilting thread, in the same color as the fabric to be quilted; thread it through a No. 8 Between needle, and knot the end. Insert the needle through the top fabric and batting, about ¾ in from the start of the quilting line; bring the needle out at the line, and pull the knot through the top, losing it in the layer of batting.

Quilt with running stitches, using the index finger of the hand below the quilt to push the needle back up to the surface, and wearing a thimble on the middle finger of your top (sewing) hand to push it back and your thumb to press down the fabric ahead of the stitches. With practice, you will be able to take several stitches at a time, rocking the needle up and down with your thimbled finger before pulling the thread through. The number of stitches that you are able to take will vary according to the type and thickness of your batting, and your experience of quilting; however, the important thing is to try to maintain a rhythm of even, neat stitches.

If you have reached the end of a pattern line and still have enough thread to continue, take the needle through the filling to the next pattern line. If this is more than a needle length away, you can "travel" by bringing the needle eye up through the top layer, swiveling the needle around, and then continuing toward the next pattern line.

When quilting motifs, follow the natural flow of a curve, for example the line of a feather segment or a flower petal, rather than quilting the entire motif outline first and then the inner details.

To finish at the end of a pattern line, make a small knot close to the last stich; make a small stitch and pull the thread through to the back, anchoring the knot in the filling. If you are part of the way along a line when you run out of thread, make a backstitch and run the thread through the batting, following along the unstitched line and taking a few tiny stitches, some ¾ in apart; run the thread back through the filling and trim. The tiny stitches will be secured when you continue quilting.

FINISHING THE EDGES
Folded edges
For this popular method, first take a line of quilting around the edge – the finished quilt will extend ½ in from this line, and the unfinished edges must extend at least 1 in beyond the quilting. The batting is then trimmed to within ¼ in of the line, and the cover fabrics to 1 in.

First take the backing evenly over the batting; work around the quilt, one edge at a time, pinning as you go. Next, fold in the front, aligning it with the backing. Pin the two layers together, and finish with a double or single row of hand or machine stitching.

Self binding
Including a ¼ in seam allowance all

around, allow enough backing fabric to create the required depth of border (in other words, if the border is to be 2 in deep, the backing should extend 2¼ in beyond the intended finished edge).

Finish all edges, trimming the top to a minimum of ½ in from the outer quilted line, and the batting to the finished edge of the border. Fold in the seam allowance around the backing, and bring the backing to the front, covering the edges of the batting and top. Start with the top and bottom edges of the quilt, and then fold over the sides, either mitering or making straight folds at the corners. Secure with hand running stitches or machine stitching.

Separate binding
For this, you can either use one of the patchwork fabrics or a contrast fabric. Unless the edge is very curved, there is no need to cut the binding strip on the bias; it should be twice the finished depth of the bound edge, plus two seam allowances (½ in).

Trim all layers to the finished size; the raw edges should be at least ½ in from the outermost quilted line. Press the ¼ in seam allowance down one long edge of the binding to the wrong side, and fold over one short edge by ½ in. Then, starting in the middle of one side edge of the quilt, and matching raw edges and with right sides together (top of quilt and right side of binding), pin the binding to the quilt.

Machine the binding in position. Stitch up to the corner, decreasing the length of the stitches as you

approach the corner; at the corner, raise the presser foot and, with the needle down through the fabric layers, pivot, making a 90 degree turn before continuing down the next edge. Leave an ample tuck in the binding at the corner, to allow you to bring the binding smoothly over to the back.

Finally, overlap the folded short edge of binding with the raw short edge by about ½ in.

Bring the free, folded edge of the binding to the back of the quilt, just covering the stitching line. At the corners, fold the fabric neatly for a mitered effect, and then slipstitch the binding to the back of the quilt, using matching thread.

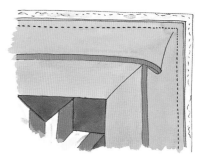

Hand-sewn Patchwork

All the quilts in this section were originally stitched by hand. The Hexagon Star quilt, which is made with backing papers, would be impossible to machine sew. However, some of the other designs, such as the Log Cabin quilt, could be machine stitched. In the case of the Crazy patchworks, you might choose, for reasons of

strength and durability, to use a mixture of hand and machine techniques. The Adirondack Star design entails lots of angled seams and many people would therefore find it easier to sew this by hand, but an experienced machinist should be able to cope.

Many people prefer the soft effect of hand-sewn seams and, even today, there are certain advantages to sewing patchwork by hand, the principal of these being that the work is more portable, and can therefore be easily carried around with you and stitched during your spare time.

ABOVE *The Adirondack Star block is one of many patchwork designs that are most easily stitched by hand.*
RIGHT *Courthouse Steps is a variation on the Log Cabin type of patchwork. The very narrow strips of fabric used here lend themselves very well to hand sewing.*

Homespun Log Cabin

Perhaps the most famous and, arguably, the most versatile of all patchwork patterns, the Log Cabin block is the basis of many quilt designs. Traditionally, the block is divided tonally into two sharply defined triangles, a light half and a dark half. The two triangles are centered on a square, which is often red, to symbolize the fire at the heart of the cabin. By joining blocks together with dark or light sections meeting, you can form strong patterns. For example, a pattern of alternating dark and light stripes running diagonally across the quilt is called Straight Furrow; rearrange the blocks so that dark and light squares, set on end, radiate out from the middle, and you have the pattern seen here, which is known as Barn Raising. There are many more variations.

Traditionally, Log Cabin designs were made with narrow strips, often cut from silks and brocades, to produce highly sophisticated and intensely colorful quilts. In contrast, the quilt featured on this page is charming in its simplicity and would not look out of place in a genuine log cabin.

On page 22 is a variation of Log Cabin known as Courthouse Steps. Instead of dividing diagonally into light and dark halves, the Courthouse Steps block divides into four (diagonally cut) quarters, the matching quarters facing each other across a central square. This piece was made with much narrower strips than the Log Cabin quilt on this page, and you might prefer to vary the quilt design by decreasing the width of the strips and adding more blocks, continuing to arrange them in the radiating pattern of the original.

RIGHT   A simple Log Cabin quilt, made from early homespun fabrics, lies on an authentic rope bed, dating back to around 1880. The Double Irish Chain quilt at the bottom of the bed echoes the red squares and surrounding red border of this attractively unsophisticated quilt.

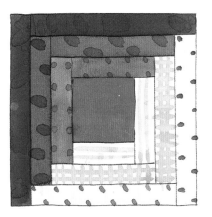

CUTTING

Note: a ¼ in seam allowance is included in all measurements. For convenience and accuracy, cut all pieces with a rotary cutter (see page 10).

Middle squares 16 pieces, 6½ in square, red fabric

Strips Cut the blue fabric and the cream and beige fabric along the straight grain into strips 2¾ in wide

Borders From the cream border fabric, cut and join lengths to make two strips 78½ x 2¼ in and two strips 82 x 2¼ in
From the red fabric, cut and join strips to make two strips 82 x 2¼ in and two strips 85½ x 2¼ in

Back of quilt From dark-blue patterned fabric, cut two pieces 85½ x 45 in

PIECING

1 Divide the fabric strips into two groups: cream (or light-colored) and blue (or dark-colored) fabrics. Take a red middle square

---

ABILITY LEVEL:

Beginner

SIZE OF FINISHED QUILT:

85½ in square

SIZE OF BLOCK:

20 in square, 16 blocks required

MATERIALS:

- 1¹⁄₁₀ yd cream patterned fabric (for inner border)
- 1½ yd red fabric
- 1 yd each of five blue (or dark-colored) patterned fabrics and five cream and beige (or light-colored) patterned fabrics
- 4¾ yd dark-blue patterned fabric (for back of quilt and self-binding)
- 88 in square piece of batting

and a strip of cream fabric. *Cut a piece from the cream strip to measure the same length as one side of the square. With right sides facing, pin and stitch the two together. Press flat.

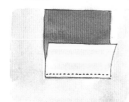

2 Take the cream strip again, and trim it to the length of the red square plus the attached cream strip. As before, pin the two layers together, stitch and press flat.

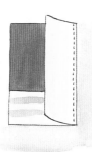

3 Take a strip of blue fabric and, working around the square, cut it to the length of the square plus the second attached strip. Pin, stitch and press flat as before.

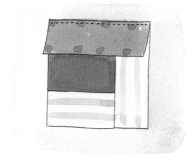

4 Take the same blue fabric and repeat the process, to complete

the first round.** Repeat from * to ** twice more to complete the first block.

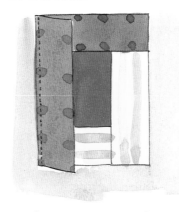

5 Make 15 more Log Cabin blocks, changing the order in which the fabrics are used in order to avoid running out of any one fabric.

6 Following the assembly diagram and taking care to arrange the pieced blocks in the same pattern of light and shade, pin together and stitch four rows of four blocks each. Join the rows in pairs and finally down the middle to make the top.

7 Next, take the two shorter lengths of cream border fabric. With right sides together, sew one length to each of the two opposite sides (top and bottom) of the pieced top. Now take the two longer strips of cream border fabric and sew one length to each of the two remaining opposite sides.

8 Take the two shorter lengths of red border fabric and sew them to two opposite sides (top and bottom) of the pieced top.

Next, sew the two longer lengths of red fabric to the remaining sides, as with the cream border.

9 Sew the two pieces of dark-blue backing fabric together down the long edges. Press the seam to one side.

10 Assemble the quilt top, batting layer and backing fabric, as directed on page 13.

FINISHING
11 Quilt along each side of the seam lines of the Log Cabin strips, the border, and the red middle square. Quilt down the middle of each Log Cabin and border strip. Select a quilting pattern from pages 123-25 (here, a simple flower pattern was used) to decorate each red middle square.

12 Next, trim the batting layer to the same size as the patchwork quilt top. Trim the dark-blue backing fabric to measure ¾ in larger all around than the pieced quilt top. Turn under a ¼ in allowance around all sides of the backing fabric and bring it over to the front of the quilt, making a self-binding, as described on page 15.

Courthouse Steps

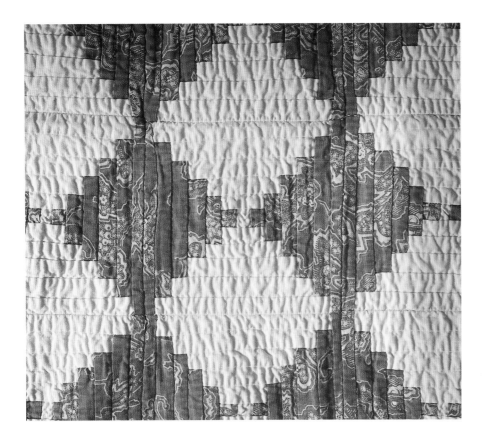

CUTTING

Note: a ¼ in seam allowance is included in all measurements. For greater convenience and accuracy, cut all pieces with a rotary cutter (see page 10).

Foundation pieces Cut 18 pieces, 6½ x 7 in, white fabric

Back of quilt Cut one piece, 34 x 19 in, white fabric

Strips Cut the remaining white and red fabrics along the straight grain into even strips, each 1 in wide

Hanging strip 17½ in touch-and-close tape and a narrow wooden batten

Note: the original piece was not padded, nor was it made into a finished object. If you wish to make a wallhanging or use the design for matching pillow covers, there is no need to add the batting layer. However, if you wish to add borders and make a crib quilt (see step 9), you will probably choose to add a layer of batting, as well as allowing extra fabric for the borders.

ABILITY LEVEL:
Intermediate

SIZE OF FINISHED PIECE:
33 x 18 in

SIZE OF BLOCK:
5½ x 6 in, 18 blocks required

MATERIALS:
- 1¾ yd white fabric
(this quantity includes enough fabric for the foundation squares and for the backing fabric)
- ⅔ yd red patterned fabric

ABOVE Cotton was used here, but silk and brocade would be effective, particularly if the design is used as a wallhanging.

PIECING

1 This design is pieced in much the same way as the Log Cabin pattern on page 18. However, in this example, the maker stitched the strips onto foundation blocks. These provide a firm base and help to strengthen the finished patchwork, especially when the strips are narrow, or when a fine fabric, such as silk, is used.

Take a foundation piece and, using a pencil and ruler, draw diagonal lines from corner to corner, marking the middle. From the white fabric, cut a piece measuring 1 in square, and baste it to the middle of the foundation piece.

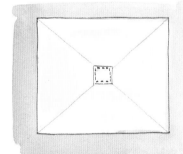

2 Take a red strip and cut two pieces, each 1 in. Stitch one to each side of the middle square, so the long edges of the combined red/white/red bar are parallel to the longer edges of the foundation piece.

3 Take a strip of white fabric and cut two pieces to the length of the red/white/red bar. Add one piece to each side. The foundation piece and the narrowness of the strips obviate the need for quilting at a later stage. However, the maker of the original piece stitched each strip twice, once on the seamline and once just inside the seam allowance, for extra security. (This is not essential.)

Continue to add pairs of red and white strips alternately, until you have a total of five pairs of white strips, on opposite sides of the central white square, and six pairs of red strips on opposite sides of the central white square.

4 Make 17 more blocks. Join them into six rows of three, positioning them with red sides together, as illustrated. The seam

allowances are ¼ in on the patchwork side, and ½ in around the foundation pieces.

5 Join the rows in groups of three and then join the two pieces together. Stitch around the outer edge on the seamline, ¼ in from the raw edge of the red fabric, then trim the white foundation fabric close to the stitching line.

6 Take the backing piece and turn in a ½ in seam allowance all around. Turn in the edges of the patchwork piece, along the stitched line. Baste and blindstitch the two together, making sure that the backing does not show on the right side.

7 To hold the backing in place, stitch invisibly along the seamlines of the rows.

8 If the finished piece is to be a wallhanging, sew one side of the touch-and-close strip to the back, ½ in down from the top edge. Sew through the backing and foundation only, not through the patchwork strips. Seal the batten to prevent the wood from staining the fabric, then glue the remaining piece of touch-and-close tape to the batten. Pin the batten to the wall, and press the piece in place.

9 If the piece is to be used for a crib quilt, plan your borders before starting. Cut two strips of (red, white, or contrasting) fabric, the length of the assembled patchwork and the finished width of the borders, plus ¾ in. Cut two strips the width of the assembled patchwork plus attached borders (desired width of quilt, plus 1 in). Cut batting to the finished size, and backing to the finished size plus ½ in all around. Attach the borders to the unbacked patchwork with ¼ in seam allowances. Assemble the layers. Quilt along seamlines, and finish as for *Folded edges* on page 15.

Hexagon Star

This English quilt exemplifies the delights and the drawbacks of the hexagon patterns so beloved of Victorian ladies. The most common design was Grandmother's Flower Garden, formed from flower-like formations in which a central hexagon is surrounded by a circle of six and then, usually, a further circle of 12 hexagons. In this particular variation, the surrounding circle is extended into a diamond shape by the addition of two extra hexagons on opposite sides of the surrounding circle.

The diamonds that are formed join naturally into stars, which can be extended and/or repeated, as in this pattern. The problems arise when it comes to creating a surrounding border that will square off the star shapes. The designer of this quilt had to make several adjustments in order to finish with an essentially square pattern, but the contrasting outer edge of white and red rosettes helps to contain the design.

The backing paper method used for quilts of this type is the most time-consuming of the various patchwork sewing methods, and this quilt should perhaps be made as a family or group venture. If time is limited, you might choose to increase the size of the hexagons and make only the central area of the quilt, omitting all, or at least some, of the border rows.

ABILITY LEVEL:
Intermediate

SIZE OF FINISHED QUILT:
104½ x 108¾ in

MATERIALS:
- ⅔ yd each of turquoise, lilac and light-brown fabrics
- 1⅓ yd each of red and moss-green fabrics
- ½ yd of dark-brown fabric
- 15½ yd white fabric (includes fabric for backing)
- ⅓ yd each of blue, navy, and yellow fabrics
- Strip of pink fabric, enough for 36 patches
- Approximately 6 yd in several (at least eight) printed and plain fabrics for rosettes
- 112 x 116 in of batting
- Templates A and B,: one for backing papers, one for patches (see page 124). If you wish to make larger hexagons, use graph paper to draw your own. (the larger template should be ¼ in larger all around than that for backing papers).

LEFT Made from dress fabrics some time around 1840, this typically English honeycomb quilt is probably the earliest in the book. The numerous patches and time-consuming technique make this type of work a labor of love, and the original maker or makers appear to have run out of steam and left backing papers basted in place.

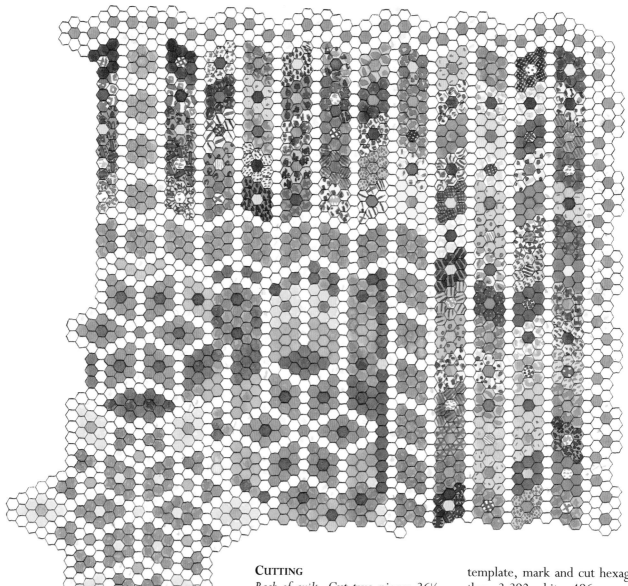

CUTTING

Back of quilt Cut two pieces 36½ x 112 in, and one piece 45 x 112 in

Backing papers Cut 8,550 templates the size of the finished patches. For speed, photocopy a page of hexagons the required number of times. As photocopies are liable to stretch, either use all photocopies or all hand-drawn shapes.

Fabric patches Using the larger template, mark and cut hexagons thus: 3,392 white; 496 moss-green; 480 red; 196 turquoise; 194 lilac; 176 light brown; 148 dark brown; 128 blue; 127 yellow; 78 navy blue; 36 pink. For the border, you will need patches for 380 diamond rosettes. Each diamond rosette takes eight hexagons (from a single fabric), plus one in a contrasting color for the middle.

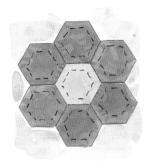

PIECING

1 Build up pattern in sections, starting from the middle as described here.

2 Prepare the patches for the middle star formation: 102 white, 57 yellow, 48 blue, 36 moss-green, six pink, and six turquoise. In each case, center a paper over the back of the patch; pin the two together, then fold the seam allowances over the paper. To ensure neat corners, you can press the allowances as you work. Baste the seam allowances, remove the pin, and press the prepared patch.

3 Take eight blue hexagons and one yellow one. Thread a needle with 13 in of quilting thread. Knot the end, then place a blue hexagon, right sides together, with a yellow one. Insert the needle through a corner of the hexagon facing you and lose the knot under the seam allowance. Using small overcast stitches, sew the patches together along one side, finishing with several stitches taken back along the stitched line.

4 Take a blue patch and join it to the first two, then continue around until you have joined a blue patch to each side of the

central yellow hexagon. Join last two hexagons to opposite sides of the resulting

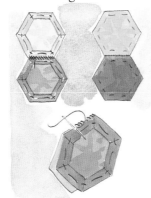

flower shape. Leave the basting stitches in place.

5 Make five more rosettes with blue patches around a yellow middle; six with yellow patches around a pink middle; and six with white patches around a turquoise middle. Make one

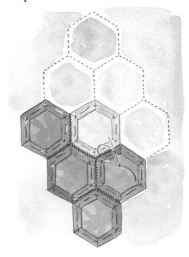

flower shape (six white hexagons around a yellow middle), then join 12 groups of three moss-green patches.

6 Join two white patches to one

side of each blue diamond rosette, then join these to the middle flower and to each other. Add the white rosettes, then the moss-green trios, then the yellow rosettes. Continue outward, adding the red star formations and the interlinking shapes.

7 Make the border rows, then add to the rest of the patchwork.

8 Remove basting stitches and papers, except those on the outside edges.

9 With the widest piece in the center, join the backing fabrics along the long edges; press seams to one side.

10 Assemble the quilt top, batting, and backing, as shown on page 15.

FINISHING

11 Contour quilt around each hexagon (except those on the edges), just inside the seamline.

12 Trim the batting to fall just short of the basted edges of the outer hexagons. Trim the backing fabric to extend ⅜ in beyond the batting.

13 Remove papers from outer patches. Re-baste seam allowances if necessary.

14 Take the backing over the edge of the batting; baste in place. Sew the top to the backing around the edges with blind stitches. Contour quilt just inside the seamline of the outer patches.

Adirondack Star

The maker of this quilt probably bought her fabrics especially for the purpose, as she went to the trouble of using a different fabric for each block. All of these fabrics, with the exception of a blue print with white polkadots, are in soft-toned pinks and beige-browns.

She must have gone to considerable lengths to find such a wide variety of coordinating fabrics – this is no rough utility quilt. The one odd blue star may be due to the fact that she could find only 35 harmonious browns and was forced to pick something different for her last choice, or it may have been a deliberate "mistake." There is an old tradition among quiltmakers of making one mistake on purpose. Sometimes a block is set in the wrong way around; sometimes you will find a patch in the wrong fabric in an otherwise exceptionally well-designed and executed quilt. This custom is found also in Islamic art, the idea being that only God can create perfection. These days,

most of us can be fairly confident of making a mistake without going to any great lengths to achieve it!

The narrow diamond, which has 45° angles at the pointed ends, is normally used to create eight-pointed stars, as opposed to the wide diamond, with 60° angles at the points, which is used for six-pointed stars and can be drawn on isometric graph paper. However, here, the narrow diamonds are set cleverly around a central square to make a twelve-pointed crown effect.

Unless you are a very skilled machinist, you will find this quilt easier to make by hand, using the running stitch method, as there are many angled seams. Individual blocks, perhaps made in silks or satins, would make attractive pillow covers and, in this case, you might prefer to use the backing paper method (see page 13), to achieve absolute accuracy.

RIGHT Combining a subtly varied range of pinkish browns, this charming American quilt dates from the 1890s. The blank center of the stars gives the design a certain lightness and sense of space, but if you choose to make the quilt in strong bright fabrics, you might prefer a contrasting color, or perhaps a dark shade, for the centers.

ABILITY LEVEL:
Experienced

SIZE OF FINISHED QUILT:
83 in square

SIZE OF BLOCK:
10¾ in square; 36 blocks
required

MATERIALS:
- 8½ yd white fabric
  (includes enough fabric for
  back of quilt)

- Printed fabrics – a separate
  fabric was used for each star
  in the original; for this, you
  require only a 4 in strip of 45
  in fabric for each block
- 83 in square piece of batting
- Templates for the following
  pieces (patterns are on page
  121, measurements do not
  include seam allowances):
  A large square; B small square;
  C triangle; and D diamond

CUTTING
Note: a ¼ in seam allowance is
included in all measurements.
Pattern pieces do not include
seam allowances.

Back of quilt Two pieces, 85 x
42¾ in, white fabric

Sashing strips Five strips (E)
3⅛ x 77¼ in, and 25 strips (F) 3⅛
x 11¼ in, white fabric

Border Two strips 3⅛ x 77¼ in,
and two 3⅛ x 83 in white fabric

PATTERN PIECES
Note: number of pieces required
for a single block are shown in
brackets.

White fabric A 36 (1), B 144 (4),
C 288 (8)

Printed fabrics D 576 (16)
(diamonds within a single block
should be the same fabric)

PIECING
1 Join two diamonds as shown,
forming a right-angled point at
one end and finishing ¼ in short of
the raw edge at each end.
Repeat, to make three more
pairs.

2 Take one pair of diamonds and stitch first one edge and then the

other to a B square (see inset seams page 12). Repeat, attaching B squares to the three remaining pairs of diamonds

3 Take a single diamond and

stitch a C triangle to one side. Take a second diamond and stitch another C triangle to one side, making a mirror image of the first piece.

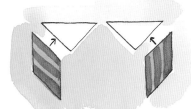

4 Stitch mirror-image pieces to each side of the double diamond corner made in step 2. Repeat steps 3 and 4 to complete the three remaining sides of the star.

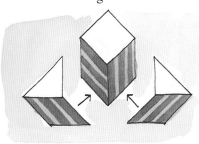

5 Stitch one side section to one side of an A square.

6 Take a second side section. Stitch it to an adjoining side of the square and then, working from the inner corner outward, stitch the seam joining the two side sections. Repeat twice more, attaching the other side sections, to complete the block.

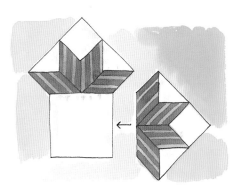

7 Make 35 more blocks in the same way, using diamonds of the same fabric within each block.

8 Using the short sashing strips, join the blocks into six rows, each row containing six blocks, separated by five sashing strips.

9 Join the rows together, putting a long sashing strip between each row of blocks. Make sure that the blocks and sashing strips of the six rows match up horizontally as well as vertically.

10 Stitch the two shorter border strips in place on each of the two opposite sides of the top. Stitch the longer border strips to the remaining two sides (top and bottom).

11 For the back of the quilt, sew the two pieces of white fabric together along the long edge and press the seam to one side.

12 Assemble the top, batting and backing together, as directed on page 13. The backing should extend beyond the other layers for 1 in all around.

FINISHING

13 Quilt each block as shown — five parallel lines across the middle square; outline quilting ¼ in in from the seamline around each diamond, a middle line down each triangle, and diagonal lines across the small square.

14 The sashing strips and borders are quilted with a trailing leaf pattern (see page 126).

15 Trim the backing to extend ⅜ in beyond the batting and the pieced top. Turn under a ¼ in allowance all around, then bring the folded edge to the front of the quilt and stitch in place (see page 15, *Self binding*).

Doll's Quilt

This doll's quilt is so simple to make that it would be an ideal first project for a child. Indeed, the original seen here may well have been made by a child. If necessary, you could easily alter the dimensions to fit a specific doll's bed or a cradle by adding to or reducing the number of patches.

Instead of being quilted in the usual fashion, this simple quilt has been tied with yarn at the intersections of the patches, although there is a little basic quilting around the borders. Tying is a sensible alternative method of holding layers together where the fabrics, like those used here, might prove too bulky to quilt, particularly across the seams.

The original quilt was made with scraps of wool cloth, giving it a cozy warmth. However, if you are planning to alter the size in order to make a crib quilt, it might be practical to select cotton fabrics – such as brushed cotton – that can be laundered easily.

ABILITY LEVEL:
Beginner

SIZE OF FINISHED QUILT:
15 x 39 in

MATERIALS:
- ⅔ yd of fabric for backing and self-binding
- Scraps for 48 patches, (each 3½ in square)
- 15 x 39 in piece of batting
- Gray crochet cotton for the ties, and a chenille needle

ABOVE The 1930s doll's quilt on the buttermilk-blue schoolmaster's desk was made from wool scraps and tied with yarn. A quilt of this type would make an ideal first project for a child, and the shape could be adapted to make a small crib quilt for a baby.

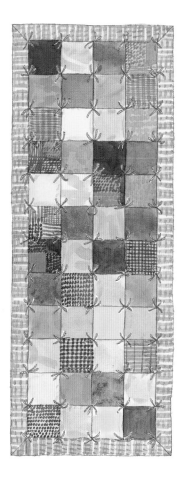

CUTTING

Note: a ¼ in seam allowance is included in all measurements. If the quilt is to be made from wool scraps, increase the seam allowance to ½ in to allow for possible fraying (especially if the quilt is to be made by a child). To reduce bulk, trim across the corners after piecing.

Back of quilt Trim backing fabric to measure 18½ x 42½ in

Patches From oddments of fabric, cut 48 patches, each 3½ in square

PIECING

1 Lay out your selected fabric patches on a large, flat surface and arrange them into 12 rows of four patches each. Alter the positions until you achieve an attractive balance of colors and textures.

2 With right sides together and raw edges even, stitch the patches into 12 short (four-patch) rows. Press the seams flat.

3 Taking care to match seams, join the 12 rows of patches together until the top is complete.

4 Assemble the quilt top, batting and backing, following the directions given on page 13 and leaving an even amount – 3½ in – of backing fabric extending beyond the other layers.

5 Turn under and press a ¼ in seam allowance all around the backing fabric. Bring the pressed edges over the top of the pieced quilt in order to cover the raw edges of the patches along both short sides. Pin and baste. Repeat this process with the long sides, and then slipstitch in place all around.

This is how the original quilt was finished. For a neater appearance, you may prefer to make mitered folds at the corners, as seen in the assembly diagram (see page 15).

6 Stitching through all layers (binding, batting, binding), stitch around the binding, 1 in from the outer edge of the quilt.

FINISHING

7 Tie the quilt layers together at every patchwork intersection and where patchwork seams meet the binding (52 ties altogether). For each tie, cut a length of crochet cotton and thread a chenille needle with a double

thickness. Starting from the top, take the needle through all layers, leaving an end about 1¼ in long on the top. Take the needle back up, close to the first hole, and then down again. Bring it back up a second time. Trim the thread to the same length as the other end. Making a square knot, tie the ends together and trim to 1 in.

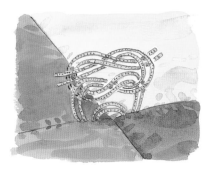

Crazy Quilt and Bear

The crazy quilt evolved as a way of making use of every last possible scrap of fabric that could be rescued from worn-out clothes, blankets or covers, at a time when the Navigation Acts, designed to protect England's trading monopolies, forbade the American colonists either to import from any country but England, or to manufacture their own textiles.

By the late 19th century, all this had changed; silk, satin, and velvet were on offer in abundance, in addition to the ordinary cotton and wool, and the crazy quilt became popular in both England and the United States. Young ladies of leisure made elaborate, colorful, and not always artistic quilts from rich and luxurious fabrics. The patches were stitched together with all manner of embroidery stitches, and the larger patches were often embellished with embroidered motifs or hand-painted designs.

The quilt seen here is more restrained than many of these Victorian crazies, partly because it was made from patchwork blocks, rather than one disorganized expanse, and partly because the colors have been carefully chosen to blend. The quilt has been hand-stitched but, if you have a machine with a facility for satin and other embroidery stitches, you could make a very attractive machine-stitched example.

The charm of the Victorian teddy bear on page 38 lies partly in the hand embroidery. However, if you are making him for a child, make sure that you secure the patches with machine stitching and add the hand embroidery for decoration only.

LEFT Made around 1910, this utilitarian quilt combines large patches in harmonizing colors. The blocks are linked by cream stitches which impose unity on the design. The room setting is in Bull Cottage, in the Adirondack Museum.

ABILITY LEVEL:
Beginner

SIZE OF FINISHED QUILT:
84 x 72 in

SIZE OF BLOCK:
12 in square, 42 blocks
required

MATERIALS:
- Assorted cotton and wool
  fabrics (no precise quantities
  can be given, as this is a true
  scrapbag project)
- 5¼ yd firm cotton,
  for foundation squares
- 4¼ yd colored cotton fabric,
  for back of quilt
- 88 x 76 in piece of batting
- Crochet cottons to contrast
  with the patchwork fabrics
- Templates for the following
  pieces. Measurements include
  seam allowances:
  A: 13 in square
  B: 12 in square

CUTTING

Back of quilt Two pieces, 44 x 74 in

Foundation squares Using either template A, or a rotary cutter, cut 42 foundation squares from firm cotton.

Batting Using template B or a rotary cutter, cut 42 squares from batting.

PIECING

1 Take a foundation square and center a wadding square over it. Pin and then baste the wadding to the foundation square with diagonal lines from corner to corner, and horizontal and vertical lines from mid-point to mid-point. For each line of basting, start from the middle and work out in each direction.

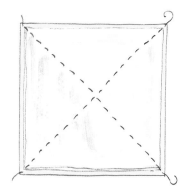

2 With your patchwork fabrics pressed and arranged beside you, cut one patch. Trim the two outer edges to fit the corner of the foundation square, then pin and baste the patch in position. The size of the finished block will be the size of the batting square, so note that edge patches will run into the seam allowance.

3 Cut a second patch, from a different fabric, and lay this next to and overlapping the first. Press a ¼ in hem down the overlapping edge. Pin and baste the second patch so that the folded edge overlaps the raw edge of the first patch.

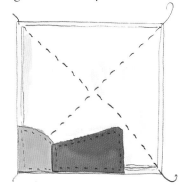

4 Continue in this way, overlapping raw edges with folded edges, until the entire foundation square has been covered, trimming the edges to the shape of the square. Check that the foundation fabric does not show through at any point, and that all patches are securely basted, then secure the patches in position with an embroidery stitch, such as feather stitch or herringbone, but leave one central patch to be secured at a later stage (see step 9).

5 Make 41 more crazy blocks.

6 Taking a ⅓ in seam allowance (the seamlines close up against the batting), join crazy blocks into seven rows of six blocks, and then join the rows. Take care to match block seams carefully.

7 Join the two back pieces together along one long edge and press the seam to one side. Assemble the back and quilt top together, as directed on page 13 for an ordinary quilt, basting thoroughly.

8 Trim the back to the same size as the quilt top, and then turn the edges of both the top and the back in, taking a ½ in seam allowance. Press and baste, and then neatly slipstitch the edges together, all around the quilt.

9 Using a contrasting thread color, feather stitch along all block seamlines, stitching through all layers. Finally, secure the remaining central patch of each block in the same manner.

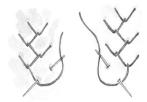

Feather Stitch

Herringbone Stitch

Crazy Bear

ABILITY LEVEL:
Beginner

SIZE OF FINISHED PIECE:
Approximately 18 in in height

MATERIALS:
- Fabric scraps, such as cotton, velvet, or wool fabrics, for patchwork
- 24 in firm, unbleached cotton fabric
- Polyester filling
- Two purchased button eyes
- Purchased black nose
- 24 in black velvet ribbon, ¾ in wide, for a neck tie
- Crochet cotton, or stranded embroidery floss, for decorative stitches
- Pattern pieces - see page 122 (seam allowances are not included, see instructions above right and on page 10).

ABOVE The cheerful teddy with the expansive embrace was made in Pennsylvania in about 1880, around the same time as the crazy quilt on which he is sitting.

Scale up the pattern pieces, and cut one of each from heavy paper. Use the paper pattern pieces to mark the outlines on fabric, then add a ½ in seam allowance around each piece when cutting out.
Note: one square = ⅜ in
Back – cut one
Front – cut two (matching pair)
Ears – cut four (two matching pairs)
Side head – cut two (matching pair)
Head centerpiece – cut one
Foot pad – cut two
Upper foot – cut four (two matching pairs)

1 Scale up the pattern pieces on page 122, and make a paper pattern for each shape (seam allowances are not included).

2 Using a hard pencil, mark each shape on the firm cotton fabric, leaving 1 in between shapes to allow for seam allowances. Make sure that pairs – i.e., side head pieces – are marked as mirror images, i.e. a left and a right side. Cut out the pieces, adding a ½ in seam allowance around each shape.

3 Using the method described for the Crazy Quilt, but without the batting layer, and laying the patches on the unmarked side of each piece, cover each shape with crazy patchwork. Secure the patches in position; if you are making the bear for a child, use a matching thread to secure the patches first with machine or hand running stitches, before adding embroidery stitches.

4 When the pieces are prepared, tack a line of staystitching around each piece, following the marked outline. Trim seam allowances to ¼ in.

5 With right sides together, join the two body front pieces along the front seamline, following the marked outline. Join the body front and back pieces together.

6 Join the two pairs of upper foot pieces, then join one upper foot to each foot pad, matching dots. Sew a foot to each leg end.

7 Turn the main body right side out and insert the filling, using a knitting needle to push the filling into the feet to make sure they are padded firmly.

8 Matching dots, and with right sides together, sew one side head piece to each side of the head centerpiece. Turn right side out and fill firmly. Turn in the raw edges along the neck edge of the head and of the body and stitch them together all around.

9 Next, stitch the teddy's eyes in position, starting and finishing the threads so that the stitches will be covered when the ears are in position, see above.

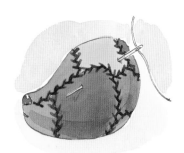

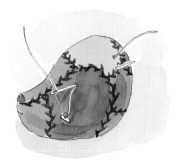

10 With right sides together and raw edges even, join the two pairs of ears, leaving the straight edge open in each case. Turn right side out and fill lightly. Turn in the raw edges and stitch the ears in position on the head.

11 Tie the velvet ribbon in a bow around the neck to finish.

Machine-sewn Patchwork

The development of mass-production of the household sewing machine coincided with that great flowering of block patchwork patterns that took place in the United States in the latter half of the century. It is incorrect to imagine that there is something more "authentic" about hand-sewn patchwork; the Modern Woman of the Victorian era was proud of her mastery of this technical advance, and many antique patchwork quilts were expertly machine-sewn. Quilts were, after all, made to serve a very practical purpose, and machine-sewn seams are much stronger than hand-sewn ones.

Apart from greater durability, and therefore washability, machine sewing has the advantage of speed. Particularly if you are new to quilting, you might enjoy starting with a simple, quick-to-sew project, such as the Schoolhouse design, before moving to a more complex pattern.

ABOVE *Quick and easy machine sewing techniques make this a deceptively simple quilt to stitch.*
RIGHT *A Canadian star coverlet, machine-sewn in the 1890s, has been draped over a table. One of the joys of making quilts, particularly machine-stitched ones, is that you can afford to use them more roughly than valuable antiques.*

Durham Basket

There are many variations on the basket pattern, some appliqué, some patchwork, and some, like this design in which the handle is applied, a mixture of both. Sometimes the basket might be of patchwork filled with applied fruits and flowers. Indeed, there is space beneath the handle of this particular basket to allow an applied filling.

This quilt was made in Durham in the North of England around the turn of the 20th century. It was quilted by Elizabeth Sanderson, who was famous for her quilting patterns. Quilting was a highly esteemed skill in the North of England – more so than patchwork – and wholecloth quilts, made to display an elaborate quilting design, were prized possessions. Elizabeth Sanderson was one of the most famous of a small group of professional quilt designers or stampers who, for a fee, would mark a quilting design onto a wholecloth quilt.

Each stamper had his or her individual patterns and designs, as well as using traditional motifs. Quilts stamped by Elizabeth Sanderson, distinguishable by their blue markings, are highly prized collectors' items.

Although the quilt here has the baskets running vertically along its length, it could equally well be made with the basket handles meeting down the middle and the deep, white borders falling at the sides of the bed. These borders obviously gave Elizabeth Sanderson the opportunity to display her quilting skills, but they could easily be trimmed to alter the size and shape of the quilt.

ABILITY LEVEL:
Intermediate

SIZE OF FINISHED QUILTS:
76 x 98 in

SIZE OF BLOCK:
9⅞ in square, 30 pieced blocks and 20 plain

MATERIALS:
• 8½ yd white fabric

(includes fabric for back of quilt)
• 1½ yd red fabric
• 78 x 100 in batting

LEFT These two turkey-red and white quilts were both made in Durham, England. The Circles and Crescents quilt on the right was made in 1850, while the Basket design on the left was quilted by Elizabeth Sanderson around 1900.

CUTTING

Note: a ¼ in seam allowance is included in all measurements; pattern pieces do not include a seam allowance.

Back of quilt 2 pieces, 39¾ x 100 in, white fabric

Plain blocks Twenty 10⅜ in (G) squares, white fabric

Side triangles For side triangles (H), cut nine 10¾ in squares from white fabric, then cut diagonally in two to make 18 triangles

Corner triangles Cut one 10⅞ in square from white fabric (I), then cut diagonally in four

Borders From white fabric, cut two J strips, 8¼ x 70½ in, and two K strips, 4¼ x 100 in

Pattern pieces Note: number of pieces for a single block are shown in brackets.
A: 420 red, 300 white (14 red, 10 white);
B: 30 matching pairs white (2);
C: 30 red (1);
D: 30 white (1);
E: 30 white (1);
F*: 30 red(1).
Patterns are on page 123.
*F is the basket handle, which is appliquéd to the block. Cut the template for this piece to the size of the finished piece, without seam allowances. Mark the shape on the right side of the fabric, and add a ¼ in seam allowance during cutting out.

PIECING

1 Sew nine white A triangles to nine red A triangles.

2 Join three squares together, so that the white and red halves are in the order shown. Add a red A triangle to one end and a white one to the other. Make another row of squares and add a red triangle to one end. Join two more squares, add a red triangle, then join a red triangle to a square.

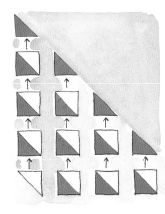

3 Join the first row to the second and so on, finishing with a single red A triangle, to complete the main body of the basket.

4 Attach the basket base (C) to the body of the basket. Join a white D triangle below the base.

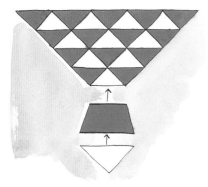

5 Stitching out each way from the corner, attach a B piece to each side of the basket.

6 Stitch a white E triangle to the top of the basket. Take the handle (F), and, using the marked outline as a guide, sew a line of small running stitch, just beyond the marked line and within the seam allowance. Clip across the top (outward) corner to reduce bulk, and take small notches from the seam allowance on the inward-facing curve.

7 Following the marked outline, turn, press, and baste the seam allowance to the wrong side, all around the handle. Carefully pin the handle in place on the block. Take a length of matching thread

and, knotting one end, sew the handle in place with small, evenly spaced stitches, losing the knot in the seam allowance and taking the needle through the seam fold as you stitch.

8 Make 29 more basket blocks in the same manner.

ASSEMBLY

9 Following the assembly diagram, arrange the patchwork blocks in rows of five, placing each block on end, and interspersing the rows of patchwork with rows of plain G blocks. Note that the patchwork blocks are positioned so that the three bottom rows have the base nearest to the bottom of the quilt, and the three top rows have the base nearest to the top, so that the handles almost meet at the middle of the quilt. Finish the plain rows with side triangles (H), and the bottom and top rows with corner triangles (I).

10 Sew the blocks together in diagonal rows, beginning with the long central rows and starting and finishing each row with an H or I triangle, as appropriate.

11 Sew the rows together, matching seams carefully, and again starting with the middle rows and working out. Add the remaining I triangles to complete the quilt top.

12 Sew a border strip (J) to the top and bottom of the quilt, then sew the remaining border strips (K), one to each side.

13 Join the two pieces for the quilt back down the long edge. Press seam allowance to one side.

14 Assemble the quilt top, batting, and backing, as directed on page 13.

FINISHING

15 Quilt across the plain blocks in a grid of 10 lines each way, running parallel to the sides of the block. Contour quilt along the inside of each shape.

16 The spaces inside the handle and on each side of the basket are filled with flowers. Using the smaller template on page 126, arrange the flowers so that some are partly hidden inside the basket.

17 The border panels are quilted with large flowers (templates are on page 125). Leave ½ in within what will be the finished outer edge unquilted, to allow for finishing.

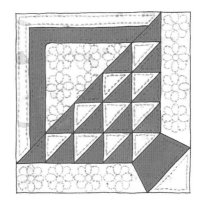

18 Trim the batting to within ¼ in of the outer quilting line, and the top and back to within 1 in of this. Finish with a *Folded edge*, as directed on page 15.

Ocean Waves

This pattern, developed towards the end of the 19th century, can be made as here, with one large block. Alternatively, you can combine two smaller blocks, one called Ocean Waves and the other (in which triangles meet in a swirling pattern at the middle) called Windmill. The maker of this quilt had a flair for design. She used the larger, single block, but emphasized the windmill effect by incorporating many similar fabrics and arranging them to meet and rotate at the "windmills" in subtle changes of color that undulate across the quilt. The result is all the more wave-like because the fabrics are so close in color and tone.

The actual stitching of this quilt is not complicated – simply a question of cutting out and then stitching the large number of triangles accurately – but, because of the clever use of color, it is important when making blocks that you put the colors in the correct order. This takes time and trouble, but the result is well worth the extra care required.

This pattern has been simplified to use only five colored fabrics, but it would be relatively easy to incorporate more, provided you study the assembly diagram closely and make sure that the color order of the blocks is adjusted correctly.

ABILITY LEVEL:
Experienced

SIZE OF FINISHED QUILT:
93½ x 99 in

SIZE OF BLOCK:
11¾ in square, 24 complete blocks, 16 half blocks

MATERIALS:
- 11½ yd white fabric (includes fabric for back of quilt)
- Five fabrics for patchwork: 28 in fabric 1; 24 in fabric 2; 26 in fabric 3; 16 in fabric 4; 26 in fabric 5
- 12 in coordinating fabric for binding
- 93½ x 99 in piece of batting
- Template for triangle A (template pattern is on page 124, measurements do not include seam allowances)

RIGHT Made in West Virginia in the 1890s, this beautifully stitched quilt features a subtly chosen and coordinated choice of navy-blue fabrics offset with crisp white.

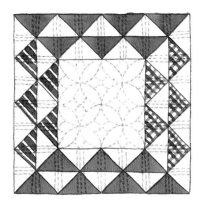

CUTTING

Note: a ¼ in seam allowance is included in all measurements, template pattern does not include a seam allowance.

Back of quilt Two pieces, 26 x 99 in, and one fabric width 45 x 99 in, white fabric

Border Two pieces 3⅜ x 99 in, two 6½ x 88½ in, white fabric

Binding Cut ten strips, each 1½ in wide across the full width (45 in) of the co-ordinating fabric. Stitch the strips together so that binding measures 11 yd.

Pattern pieces
Fabric 1: 180 A triangles
Fabric 2: 156 A triangles
Fabric 3: 168 A triangles
Fabric 4: 96 A triangles
Fabric 5: 168 A triangles

White fabric Cut 768 A triangles and twenty-four 8⅜ in squares (B) for middle sections of whole blocks. For half blocks, cut eight 8¾ in squares, and cut each in half diagonally to make 16 side triangles (C)

PIECING

Ocean Waves block

1 You need 24 white triangles, seven of fabric 2, five of fabric 1, seven of fabric 3, five of fabric 5 Take three white triangles and a triangle of fabric 1. Join a strip of two white triangles with a fabric 1 triangle in the middle. Add a white triangle to the top.

2 Take three triangles of fabric 2 and one white triangle. Make a

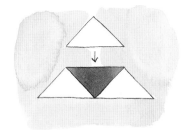

strip with two triangles of fabric 2 and a white triangle in the middle. Sew a triangle of fabric 2 to the top of the strip to complete a large triangle.

3 Take three white triangles and

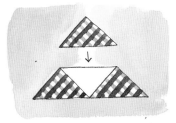

a triangle of fabric 3. Make a four-triangle piece, as in step 1.

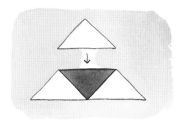

4 Repeat step 2 with three triangles of fabric 5 and one white triangle.

5 Take a white B square and stitch a pieced triangle to each side in clockwise order: fabric 1, 2, 3 and 5.

6. Take three triangles of fabric 2 and one white triangle. Make another large triangle. Repeat to make an identical large triangle.

7 Take three white triangles and one of fabric 1. Join them into a large triangle. Repeat to make an identical large triangle.

8 Make four more triangles, two consisting of three triangles of fabric 3 with one white triangle; and two consisting of three white triangles and one of fabric 5.

9 Stitch a triangle containing a fabric 5 patch to a triangle containing three fabric 2 patches. This is one corner of the Ocean Waves block.

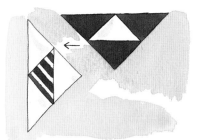

10 Stitch the corner to the appropriate side of the pieced middle section of the Ocean Waves block.

11 Make the remaining corners, joining large pieced triangles in pairs as follows: fabric 2 with fabric 1, fabric 1 with fabric 3, and fabric 3 with fabric 5. Again working clockwise, join these corners to the block. This completes one Ocean Waves block.

Ocean Waves – half blocks
12 The sides and corners are made from half blocks. Take 24 triangles: 12 white, seven of fabric 4 and five of fabric 1. Sew a row of two white triangles alternating with two of fabric 1: white/1/white/1. Make a second row in the same way. Sew the two rows together to make a parallelogram.

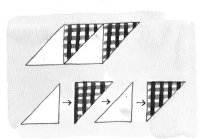

13 Make another parallelogram, this time alternating white triangles with triangles of fabric 4. Join the parallelograms to a white C triangle, the fabric 1 parallelogram on the left and the fabric 4 parallelogram on the right. You should have fabric 1 triangles adjoining one side of the triangle, and white triangles on the other side.

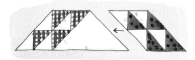

14 Following step 9, make a corner triangle, using three white triangles and a triangle of fabric 1 on one side and three triangles of fabric 4 and one white triangle on the other side. Stitch the assembled corner piece to the rest of the half block.

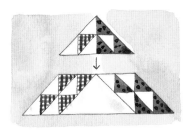

15 Assemble the remaining 23 full blocks and 15 half blocks. Each full block is made of 24 white triangles and 24 colored triangles divided into four sections. Each half block contains 12 white triangles and 12 colored triangles, which are divided equally into two sections.

For each block/half block, the number of triangles in each color are listed in brackets beside the number code for the relevant fabric. When assembling the blocks/half blocks, it is essential that you piece them in the listed order.

The blocks/half blocks are listed in assembly order, working from the top left-hand corner of the quilt, in diagonal rows, from left to right.

Corner
Fabric 1 (5), 4 (7) (the half block pieced in steps 12–14)
Fabric 2 (5), 1 (7)

Row 1
Fabric 5 (5), 3 (7)
Fabric 5 (7), 1 (5), 5 (7), 4 (5)
Fabric 3 (7), 5 (5), 2 (7), 5 (5)
Fabric 4 (5), 5 (7)

Row 2
Fabric 2 (5), 3 (7)
Fabric 2 (7), 3 (5), 2 (7), 1 (5)
Fabric 1 (7), 2 (5), 5 (7), 2 (5)
Fabric 2 (7), 3 (5), 2 (7), 1 (5)
Fabric 4 (7), 3 (5), 1 (7), 2 (5)
Fabric 2 (5), 3 (7)

Row 3
Fabric 5 (5), 1 (7)
Fabric 5 (7), 3 (5), 5 (7), 3 (5)
Fabric 1 (7), 3 (5), 4 (7), 5 (5)
Fabric 2 (7), 1 (5), 3 (7), 5 (5)
(the block made in steps 1–11)
Fabric 1 (7), 3 (5), 1 (7), 2 (5)
Fabric 5 (7), 4 (5), 3 (7), 1 (5)
Fabric 2 (7), 1 (5), 3 (7), 5 (5)
Fabric 5 (5), 1 (7)

Row 4
Fabric 1 (5), 2 (7)
Fabric 3 (7), 1 (5), 5 (7), 2 (5)
Fabric 5 (7), 3 (5), 1 (7), 4 (5)
Fabric 1 (7), 4 (5), 1 (7), 5 (5)
Fabric 2 (7), 5 (5), 4 (7), 1 (5)

Fabric 4 (7), 1 (5), 3 (7), 2 (5)
Fabric 2 (7), 4 (5), 1 (7), 3 (5)
Fabric 5 (7), 2 (5)

Row 5
Fabric 5 (5), 2 (7)
Fabric 3 (7), 2 (5), 1 (7), 2 (5)
Fabric 3 (7), 5 (5), 2 (7), 1 (5)
Fabric 5 (7) 1 (5), 4 (7) 3 (5)
Fabric 2 (7), 3 (5), 1 (7), 3 (5)
Fabric 4 (7), 2 (5)

Row 6
Fabric 1 (5), 3 (7)
Fabric 5 (7), 1 (5), 4 (7), 3 (5)
Fabric 5 (7), 3 (5), 1 (7), 4 (5)
Fabric 3 (7), 5 (5)

Bottom right corner
Fabric 4 (5), 5 (7)
Fabric 5 (5), 3 (7)

ASSEMBLY

16 Join the blocks and half blocks in diagonal rows, following the large assembly diagram on page 48 and the individual block descriptions listed in step 15.

17 Next, sew the diagonal rows together, matching seams carefully.

18 Take the two shorter, wider border strips, and join one each to the top and the bottom of the patchwork. Join a longer border strip down each side.

19 To assemble the quilt back, stitch one of the narrower pieces of white fabric to each long side of the wide, central piece. Press the seam allowances to one side.

20 Next, assemble the quilt top, batting, and backing fabric, as directed on page 15.

FINISHING

21 The main quilting lines are stitched in sets of three closely spaced parallel lines. These run down through the middle of the triangles of which this quilt is predominantly formed.

When quilting your pattern, make sure that your quilting lines stop 1 in clear

BELOW Detail of the separate binding.

of the raw edges to allow for binding.

22 The large, white middle sections of the Ocean Waves blocks are quilted in a pattern of four large flowers. Template patterns can be found on page 126).

23 To finish, bind the edges of the quilt as directed for a *Separate binding* on page 15.

Lady of the Lake

This name is given to several different blocks, perhaps because the name "Lady of the Lake" has a romantic, Arthurian ring to it, which appealed to Victorian quiltmakers. In this example, the Lady is represented by the central portion of a block known as Light and Shade. Certainly the bold, plain center, with its dramatic triangles contained in a border of smaller triangles, has an heraldic flavor.

Like several other quilts in this book, this example was made with white and red fabrics. White cotton was inexpensive and ubiquitous, and as an added bonus, white has the effect of enhancing colors. Turkey-red dye is both strong and permanent, and was used in the East for many centuries before being introduced into

America around 1830. It is easy to forget in a consumer society how simply most people lived only just over a century ago, how few possessions they had, and how much a splash of color could liven up their surroundings. These days, we have many possessions, and many patterns and colors vying for attention in our homes; our difficulty is imposing restraint and harmony upon a multiplicity of objects.

This particular quilt would look lovely set against plain furnishings in a simple, country-style setting, or as a bold statement in an otherwise minimalist city dwelling. It would look equally attractive in other colors, such as white with blue, green or black, or perhaps ocher and terracotta.

ABILITY LEVEL:
Intermediate

SIZE OF FINISHED QUILT:
76¼ x 65½ in

SIZE OF BLOCK:
10¼ in square, 42 blocks required

MATERIALS:
- 7⅓ yd white fabric (includes fabric for back of quilt)
- 1¾ yd contrast fabric
- 75¾ x 65½ in piece of batting

- Templates for the following pieces (template patterns are on page 124, measurements do not include seam allowances):
  A large triangle
  B small triangle

RIGHT Another red and white quilt, this Lady of the Lake design was made in Canada in about 1880. Make sure, particularly with a design of strong contrasts such as this, that the dyes are completely colorfast.

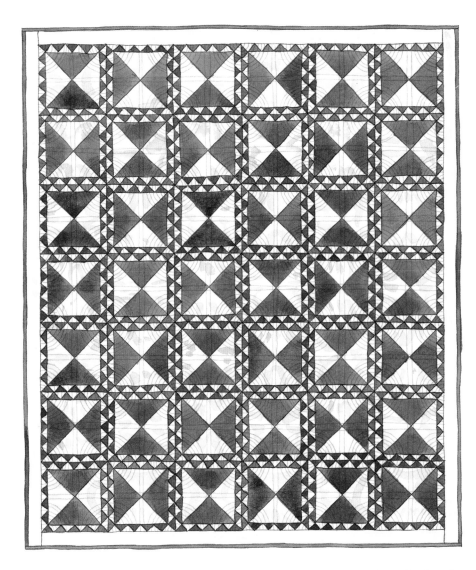

PIECING

1 Take four white B triangles and five colored ones; stitch them together as shown. Take care to match seamlines (not points, see page 13) accurately. Repeat, making a second identical strip. Join five white B triangles and four colored B triangles, repeat.

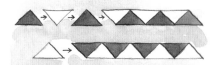

2 One by one, join each strip to a large A triangle of the appropriate color – a strip with five white triangles to a large white triangle, and vice versa. Match seamlines accurately so that the points of the smaller triangles meet the base of the larger triangle.

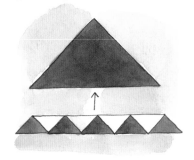

CUTTING

Note: a ¼ in seam allowance is included in all measurements, pattern pieces do not include seam allowances.

Back of quilt Two pieces, 65½ x 38⅝ in, white fabric

Border Two pieces 2½ x 66 in, and two pieces 2¼ x 76¼ in white fabric

Binding Cutting along the length of the colored fabric, cut even strips, each 1¼ in wide. Join the strips together to produce a strip 8 yd long (this includes some additional material for easing around corners).

Pattern pieces Cut 84 A triangles and 378 B triangles from white fabric, then cut the same amount from colored fabric; pattern pieces are on page 124.

3 Piece the four quarters of the block together. First, join two pairs of pieced triangles (one with a large white triangle, and one with a large colored triangle) together, then join the two halves of the block.

4 Make 41 more blocks in the same way.

5 Taking care to alternate the positioning of the white and colored triangles, as shown on the assembly diagram, join six rows of seven blocks each. Pin carefully before stitching to make sure that the points of the triangles meet exactly.

6 Join two groups of three rows, again following the assembly diagram, and then join the two halves of the patchwork together.

7 Take a short border strip and join it to one short (top or bottom) end of the patchwork. Join the other short strip to the opposite end. Now take the two longer border strips and join these in the same way to the two sides of the pieced top.

8 Stitch the two quilt back pieces together lengthwise Press the seam allowance to one side.

9 Assemble the backing, batting and top, as directed on page 13.

FINISHING

10 First quilt invisibly along the seamlines, joining the blocks together, then quilt along the inner-border seamlines, as shown.

11 Next, quilt horizontally and vertically across the middle (large triangles) of each block, using two sets of parallel lines, set ⅓ in apart.

12 Quilt eight radiating circles from the points where the blocks meet, as shown.

13 When you have finished quilting, trim the edges to neaten them, if necessary, and attach the binding around the edges (see page 15).

Sun in Splendor

This quilt, made from shiny peach and gold polished cottons is a product of the 1930s quilting revival. This resurgence of quilting was a result of the Great Depression, when women turned their hands to anything that would earn a few extra coins to feed their families. However, the warm, glowing colors and elaborate quilting of this design convey an air of luxurious opulence – there is nothing of the pioneer spirit about this quilt!

As a block, this eight-pointed star-within-a-star design is often called the St. Louis block, but Sun in Splendor, the symbol of England's Yorkist King Edward IV, seems more appropriate for this quilt from the North of England. Many star or sun patterns are built up with numerous small patches. Here the large pieces allow the emphasis to lie with the quilting pattern.

ABILITY LEVEL:
Experienced

SIZE OF FINISHED QUILT:
88 x 78 in

MATERIALS:
- 8 yd yellow polished-cotton fabric (includes fabric for back of quilt)
- 3¼ yd peach polished-cotton fabric
- 88 x 78 in piece of batting
- Templates for the following pieces (template patterns are on page 121, measurements do not include seam allowances):

  A large (peach) diamond
  B small (yellow) diamond
  C triangle
  D corner pieces

RIGHT Made in the North of England around the time of the Great Depression, this cheerful quilt, with its rays of peach and gold, was made with polished cotton, which emphasize the brightness of the colors and the elaborate quilting patterns.

CUTTING

Make the templates to the size of the finished pieces (without seam allowances); then add ¼ in seam allowances when cutting out.

Back of quilt Two pieces, 79 in long, cut across the width of the fabric, yellow fabric

Border 1 Two strips 32½ x 4 in (E), two 9½ x 4 in (F), peach fabric

Border 2 Two strips 39½ x 4½ in (G), two 47½ x 2 in (H), yellow fabric

Border 3 Two strips 42½ x 5½ in (I), two 57½ x 5½ in (J), peach fabric

Border 4 Two strips 52½ x 7½ in (K), two 71½ x 5½ in (L), yellow fabric

Border 5 Two strips 62½ x 9 in (M), two 90 x 9 in (N), peach fabric

Pattern pieces
Peach fabric: eight A diamonds; Yellow fabric: eight B diamonds, four C triangles, four D corners

same direction (either clockwise or counterclockwise).

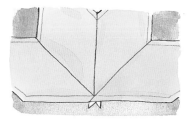

3 Stitch the two halves of the star/sun shape together. Press very carefully so that the tails interlock neatly.

4 One by one, stitch a peach-colored diamond into the V-shape between each pair of yellow diamonds. Follow the instructions on page 12 for stitching into angled seams, and stitch along marked seamlines only.

PIECING

1 Take two yellow diamonds and join them along one side. Stitch along the marked seamline only. Press the seam open. Make three more pairs.

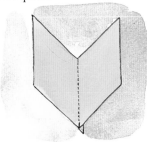

2 Join two pairs of diamonds, making half the inner shape, then join the other two pairs of diamonds. Take care to stitch accurately along the seamlines only (not into the seam allowances). Press the seams open. As you press diamonds that are seamed on both sides of the point, you will find that the seam allowances of each diamond fold over into a tail shape. When you press the seams, make sure that all the tails are facing in the

5 One by one, attach the corner pieces (D) to the central shape, again piecing as for angled seams and stitching along seamlines only. Press seams to each side.

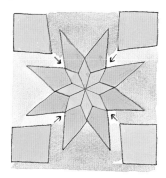

6 Join in the C triangles. As each of these is joined, the base of the triangle should run on a straight line with the adjacent edges of the corner pieces, so that you finish with a large square shape.

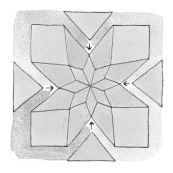

7 Attach E border strips to the top and bottom of the pieced square, then stitch F strips to both sides.

8 Stitch the remaining borders to the patchwork in the following order: G, H, I, J, K, L, M, N.

9 Join back pieces down the long edge and press seams to one side.

10 Mark the quilting pattern. In the North of England, quilting patterns were often marked using a needle; this is a particularly effective method to use when working with glazed fabrics. Lay the quilt top, right side up, on a flannel blanket; hold the template in position with one hand, and mark the quilting pattern using a blunt-ended rug needle.

When marking a border pattern, start from the middle of the border and work out in both directions, making balanced adjustments, where necessary, for neat corners.

11 Assemble the top, batting and back together, as directed on page 13.

FINISHING

12 The pieces of the inner shape – each ray of the stars and the corners and filler triangles – are contour, quilted with lines running on each side of the seamlines.

13 The corner pieces and triangles (D and C) of the inner shape and the inner border (1) are quilted in lines of cross-hatch the lines set 1¼ in apart.

14 At the middle of the yellow star is a large flower shape. This is repeated at each corner of the quilt on borders 4 and 5 (each end of border 5 strips – leave 1 in clear at outer, raw edges for finishing).

15 Each of the peach rays is quilted with a small flower, a half-flower, and a petal. The small flowers are repeated at the corners of border 2.

16 G, K and L border strips are quilted with the scroll and leaf patterns shown on pages 123-125, and H with a narrow, trailing leaf pattern. These were clearly drawn without a template on the original quilt and adapted to fit into the width of the respective borders. Each border strip features two trails; these start at the opposite corners of the strip, next to the corner flowers, the narrow leafy ends of the trails overlapping at the middle of the strip.

17 I and J borders are quilted with a cable pattern, neatly looped around at the corners.

18 The outer borders have flowers at the corners and a design of leaves and diamond crosshatching along the edges. Use the leaf template on page 125 to draw the leaf shape, filling in the middle lines/veins freehand, or with dashes cut into the template; reverse the template to draw the next leaf, and so on. Fill the spaces between leaves with lines of crosshatching set 1¼ in apart.

19 When you have completed the quilting, trim the back and front to measure ½ in larger than the batting all around. Finally, turn in the raw edges and finish as directed for *Folded edges* on page 15.

Toad in a Puddle

The second half of the 19th century saw the development of hundreds of new patchwork patterns in the United States. All of these patterns had their own names and meanings which often changed depending upon where the quiltmaker lived. For example, the Hand of Friendship block in well-developed Eastern states was called Duck's Foot in the Mud in farming communities, while the same block was known by the name of Bear's Paw by the pioneers moving west.

Patchwork patterns were named after every aspect of quiltmakers' lives. The birds that the women saw every day were very popular subjects, celebrated in such patterns as Hens and Chickens, Birds in the Air, Wild Goose Chase, Hovering Hawks, and Ducks and Ducklings. Many designs were developed to commemorate the professions of the quiltmakers' husbands, for example, Chips and Whetstones, The Anvil, Monkey Wrench, and Carpenter's Square. With many people turning to religion in times of hardship, the Bible also provided inspiration for hundreds of quilt designs.

This quilt was made from fabric scraps which is why each block is pieced in a different color combination. You can make each Toad in a Puddle block from scraps to achieve a similar effect. Alternatively, the following instructions give the required lengths for a red, white and blue quilt.

ABILITY LEVEL:
Beginner

SIZE OF FINISHED QUILT:
84 x 98 in

SIZE OF BLOCK:
10 in square (42 blocks required)

MATERIALS:
- 9 yds royal blue fabric
  (includes fabric for back of quilt)
- 3½ yds red fabric
- 3 yds white fabric
- ⅜ yd of coordinating fabric
  for binding 84½ x 98½ in
  piece of batting
- Templates for the following

pieces (measurements include seam allowances):
A, B, C triangles, see page 122.
D: 4 in square
E: 10½ in square

RIGHT Set against a backdrop of weathered wood, this 1840s quilt made in New England provides a strong accent. The quilt's elegant appearance is contradicted by the name of the design — Toad in a Puddle! During peak hours of sunlight, the curtains are drawn to keep the quilt's bright colors from fading.

in half diagonally to make a total of four corner triangles.

Binding Cut nine 1½ in wide strips across the full width of the coordinating fabric; stitch strips together so binding measures 12 yds long.

Pattern Piece	Number of Pieces
A	(12) 504 red
B	(16) 672 white
C	(4) 168 red
D	(1) 42 white

Note: The number of pieces required for a single block are given in parentheses. Patterns are on page 122.

PIECING
Toad in a Puddle Block
1 Sew one B and one reversed B to each side of A, to form a rectangle. Construct seven additional B-A-B rectangles in exactly the same manner.

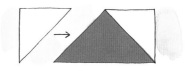

CUTTING
Note: A ¼ in seam allowance is included in all measurements; pattern pieces do not include a seam allowance.

Back of quilt Two pieces, 42½ x 98½ in, royal-blue fabric.

Plain blocks 30 E squares, royal-blue fabric.

Side triangles For side F triangles, cut five 15¼ in squares from royal-blue fabric; cut each square diagonally into four to make 20 side triangles. Use one triangle as a pattern to cut two additional triangles, for a total of 22 F triangles.

Corner triangles For corner G triangles, cut two 7⅞ in squares from royal-blue fabric, then cut

2 Sew two B-A-B rectangles together, making sure that the A triangles point in the same direction, then sew a single A triangle to the B-B edge as shown. Repeat three more times to produce a total of four patchwork strips.

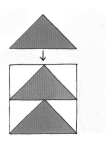

3 Sew a C triangle to each side of a patchwork strip, forming a triangle, as shown below. Repeat once more to produce two identical patchwork triangles.

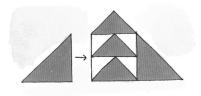

4 Sew the remaining two patchwork strips to each side of a D square as shown, in order to create the central strip of the block.

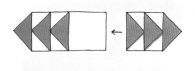

5 To complete the Toad in a Puddle block, sew a patchwork triangle to each side of the central strip, taking great care to match the seams carefully in the middle.

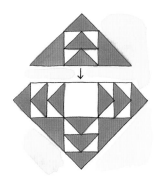

6 Construct 41 more Toad in a Puddle blocks in the same way.

ASSEMBLY
7 Follow the Quilt Plan. Work on a flat surface. Arrange the patchwork blocks with the plain E blocks to form a checkerboard pattern. The quilt has seven horizontal rows of blocks, with six blocks in each row.

8 Fill in the sides of the quilt top with the F triangles and the corners with the G triangles.

9 Sew the blocks together in diagonal rows, starting with the long middle rows and working outward to each corner. Do not forget to add an F or G triangle to each end of each row.

10 Sew the rows together, matching the seams carefully. Sew the remaining two G triangles to each unfinished corner to complete the quilt top.

11 To construct the quilt back, sew the two fabric pieces together along the long edges. Press the seam allowance to one side (this will make it stronger than an open seam and will help to hold the filling in).

12 Assemble the quilt top, batting and backing as directed on page 13.

FINISHING
13 Outline-quilt the A and C triangles on each block. Quilt an "X" across each D square as shown on the Block Plan.

14 Quilt each plain square with a pattern echoing the patchwork.

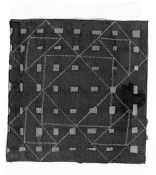

15 Quilt a quarter-pattern of the patchwork in each F triangle.

16 Quilt a triangle ½ in away from edges of each G triangle.

17 Bind the quilt with a *Separate binding*, as directed on page 15.

Bordered Chain

One of the delights of antique quilts is their individuality; no two are identical, and small details often give a strong impression of the maker's personality and circumstances. The middle panel of this striking quilt appears to have started life as a crib quilt. The red dye has faded and the fabrics are worn with much washing, but this was clearly a much-loved piece — perhaps a "comfort blanket" — and could not go to waste. Economy may also have been a factor, but this is no plain utilitarian piece, and at a time when most people had to "turn every penny over twice", the maker — or re-maker — went to considerable expense as well as effort.

Instead of surrounding the crib quilt with plain borders, the maker decided to use patchwork borders that would be in keeping with the character of the original. Although it is very attractive, the result is slightly eccentric, since the triangles and rectangles of the border strips tend to dominate the central patches. The idea of reworking a quilt in this manner was — and still is — a good one, and it has certainly prolonged the life of a beautiful piece of patchwork.

The original crib quilt was considerably longer than it was wide — 13 blocks down the length of the quilt compared with nine across the width. In order to produce a square-shaped quilt, the maker has added borders of varying widths, the side strips being generally wider than those at the top and bottom.

ABILITY LEVEL:

Intermediate

SIZE OF FINISHED QUILT:

87¾ x 87 in

SIZE OF BLOCK:

4 in square, 58 plain blocks and 59 patchwork required

MATERIALS:

- 11½ yd white fabric (this includes enough fabric for the back of the quilt)
- 3⅔ yd red fabric
- 87¾ x 87 in piece of batting
- Templates for the following pattern pieces:
  A 2½ in square;
  B 1½ in square;
  C 1½ x 2½ in
- Templates for the following pattern pieces (templates are given on page 121, measurements do not include seam allowances): D, E, F, G, H, I, K, L

LEFT *This eccentric design, made in Durham in about the 1890s, shows how ingenious quiltmakers could be in adapting borders to achieve the desired shape and make the best use — and re-use — of their materials.*

CUTTING

Note: a ¼ in seam allowance is included in all measurements; pattern pieces do not include a seam allowance.

Back of quilt Two pieces, 45⅛ x 44 in, white fabric

Plain blocks Fifty-eight 4½ in squares, white fabric

Pieced blocks Fifty-nine 2½ in squares (A) and 1½ in squares (B), all red fabric; 236 rectangles 1½ x 2½ in (C), white fabric

Border 1 Two 52.5 x 8½ in strips, red fabric

Border 2 Two 52½ x 5½ in strips, red fabric

Border 5 Two 58½ x 4¾ in strips, white fabric

Border 6 Two 77 x 6¾ in strips, white fabric
Border 9 Two 88 x 1⅞ in strips, red fabric

Border 10 Two 88¾ x 4 in strips, red fabric

Pattern pieces
Border 3 Cut four D triangles, red fabric; 16 F triangles, red fabric; and 18 F triangles, white fabric

Border 4 Cut four D triangles, red fabric; 18 F triangles, red fabric; and 20 F triangles, white fabric

Border 7 Cut four I triangles, white fabric; 56 G triangles, red fabric; and 26 H parallelograms, white fabric

Border 8 Cut four J triangles, white fabric; 76 K triangles, red fabric; and 36 L parallelograms, white fabric

PIECING

Chain block
1 Take two small red B squares and sew one to each short side of a white C rectangle.

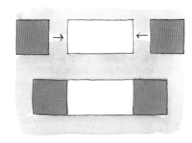

Repeat with two more red B squares.

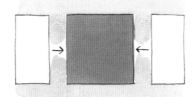

2 Sew a white C rectangle to each side of a large red A

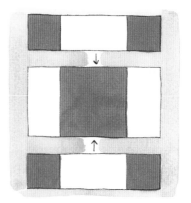

square, as shown.

3 Stitch the three strips together, see above.

4 Make 58 more identical blocks in the same way.

5 Following the assembly diagram, join the blocks together in rows, as follows. First make a row of five pieced blocks alternating with four plain-white blocks. Repeat to make six more identical rows. Now make a row of five plain blocks alternating with four pieced ones and repeat five times. Join the rows of blocks together, making two sections, one with six rows and one with five rows. Join the two sections together to complete the middle section of the quilt.

6 With right sides together, stitch a 52½ x 8½ in strip of red fabric (border 1) to each long side of the pieced center. Next, stitch a 52.5 x 5½ in strip of red fabric (border 2) to the remaining top and bottom edges of the pieced center.

Border 3

7 Stitch a red D triangle to a white E triangle to make a

parallelogram. Make a second, mirror-image D/E patch, for the opposite end of the row.

8 Stitch a red E triangle to a white E triangle, joining the short edges. Add more E

triangles, alternating colors and inverting the triangles to make a band of eight red and seven white triangles.

9 Add a corner piece made in step 7 to each end of the row.

10 Make a second strip, for the opposite border, in the same way.

Border 4

11 Join a D triangle to a white F triangle, in the same way as the D/E piece made in step 7. Repeat to make a mirror-image piece for the opposite end of the row.

12 Join eight red F triangles to seven white ones, alternating the colors and inverting the triangles, as in step 8. Add a corner piece to each end. Make a second

border strip in the same way.

Border 7

13 Stitch an I triangle to a G triangle, short sides together. Make an inverted piece to match

– these will be the end sections of one border strip – then join another pair of I/G pieces, completing the end sections of the opposite border strip.

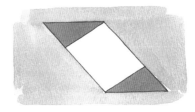

14 Take a white H parallelogram

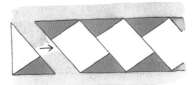

and stitch a red G triangle to each short side, making a longer parallelogram, as shown in the diagram. Make 25 more pieces in the same way.

15 Join an I/G piece to a G/H/G parallelogram.

16 Add a further 12 parallelograms, then join on a mirror-image I/G piece to complete the opposite end of the border strip.

17 Make the second, opposite border strip in the same way.

Border 8

18 Stitch a J triangle to a K triangle, joining the short sides, as shown for the I/G end sections described in step 13. Make an inverted piece to match, then join another pair of J/K pieces, completing the end sections of both border strips.

19 Take a white L parallelogram and stitch a red K triangle to each short side, making a longer parallelogram, as for border 7, step 14. Make 35 more pieces in the same way.

20 Join a J/K piece to a K/L/K parallelogram; add 17 more parallelograms, and then a mirror-image J/K piece. The method is exactly the same as when completing the side border strips, described in steps 15-17. Make the second border strip in the same way.

ASSEMBLY

21 Pin and stitch the pieced border 3 strips to the top and bottom of the central patchwork, taking care to match the corners exactly where they should fall in the seamlines (¼ in in from the raw edges)

22 Pin and stitch pieced border 4 strips, one to each side, in the same way, then neatly join the two adjacent edges of the D triangles at each corner, to make a mitered effect.

23 Stitch a 58½ x 4¾ in strip of white fabric (border 5) to the top and bottom of the quilt, then stitch a 77 x 6¾ in strip of white fabric (border 6) to each side.

24 Stitch a pieced border 7 strip to each side of the quilt.

25 Stitch a pieced border 8 strip to the top and base of the quilt.

26 Stitch a 88 x 1⅞ in strip of red fabric (border 9) to top and bottom of quilt.

27 Stitch a 88¼ x 4 in strip of red fabric (border 10) to each side of the quilt.

28 Join the two backing fabrics along the long edge and press the seam allowances to one side.

29 Assemble the top, batting and backing as directed on page 14.

FINISHING
30 This cover was quilted in zigzags, set 1 in apart. You could vary this by outline quilting the pieced blocks and borders; quilt flower designs in the plain blocks; quilt a chain down borders 1 and 2 and a zigzag in borders 5 and 6 to echo the triangles of borders 3 and 4, and finish with a trailing leaf down border 10. Whatever design you choose, leave 1 in around the outer edge for finishing.

ABOVE A selection of quilts displaying the wide variety of quilting patterns.

31 Finish with *Folded edges* (see page 15), taking care that no white fabric shows on the front.

Schoolhouse

An endearing and enduringly popular design, the Schoolhouse block was developed during the 1870s, at a time when the school, along with the church and the local store, formed a focal point of community life. Variants of the block include Old Kentucky Home and Little Red House. The name and the simple, cozy look of the little houses, makes this an ideal design for a child.

Pictorial blocks are comparatively few in number, in contrast to the huge number of geometric designs in existence. This scarcity is largely because patchwork does not lend itself readily to representational images; the simplicity of this house shape is the key to its success.

The fabrics here are used cleverly to add to the image. The strong checked pattern of the roofs conveys an impression of tiles; the muted browns and grays of the walls give the effect of color-washed plaster; while the fabrics for the windows are ideal for suggesting panes of glass and, at the side, a shade.

ABILITY LEVEL:
Beginner

SIZE OF FINISHED QUILT:
75 x 59½ in

SIZE OF BLOCK:
13 in square, 20 blocks required

MATERIALS:
- 4⅓ yd yellow fabric for sashing strips and back of quilt
- 75 x 59½ in piece of batting
- Cream-colored yarn for ties

Patchwork fabrics:
Note: In the original quilt, the schoolhouses are identical, except for the walls; the quantities listed are adequate for all the blocks, except the amount for the walls, which is ample for a single house.
Sky, roof, and house edging ¾ yd pale striped fabric
Chimneys 8 in red fabric
Roofs ⅔ yd brown gingham-type check
Walls for each house, 4 in plain fabric in brown or gray
Front windows ⅓ yd fabric with cross-lined pattern
Side windows ⅓ yd striped fabric

- Templates for the following pieces (see page 124. Seam allowances not included):
A and C sky
B chimneys
E roof
D, F, G, I, J, L and M walls
K front windows
H side window
O and N roof and house edging

RIGHT Made in Vermont in about 1880, this delightful quilt was hand-stitched and then tufted rather than quilted. The carefully chosen fabrics emphasize the country-style imagery, and the yellow sashing strips add to the cheerful, cozy feeling of the design.

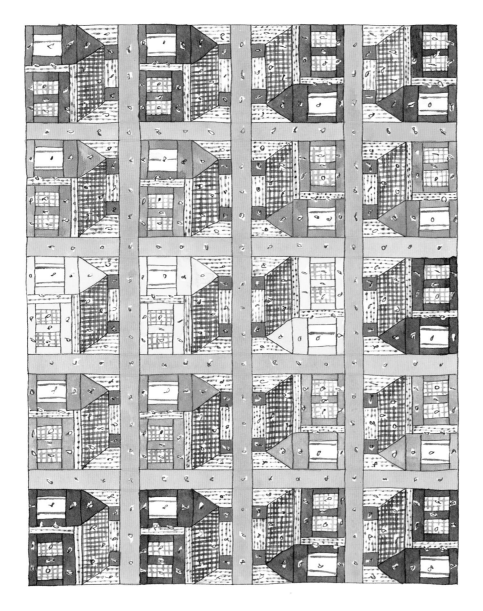

J 60 (three for each house),
L 20, M 20.Roof fabric E 20
Side window fabric H 20
Front window fabric K 40

PIECING

Schoolhouse block

1 Stitch a chimney (B) to each
side of a straight C sky strip.

2 Sew a triangular wall piece (D)
to the left side of an E roof piece

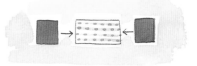

3 Join the chimney/sky strip to
the top ridge of the roof. Piece

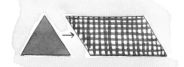

in an A sky section
to each side Starting from
the peak of the roof, stitch
along the side edge, following
the instructions for angled
seams (page 12) Return to
the roof peak and stitch
around the three sides of the
chimney.

CUTTING

Note: a ¼ in seam allowance is
included in all measurements.
Pattern pieces do not include a
seam allowance.

Back of quilt Two pieces,
76 x 30½ in, yellow fabric

Sashing strips Four 76 x 3 in

strips (P), and sixteen 13½ x 3in
strips (Q), yellow fabric

Pattern pieces
Sky, roof, and house edging
fabric A 40, N 20, O 20
Brick-red fabric B 40
Sky fabric C 20
Assorted wall fabrics D 20, F 20,
G 40 (two for each house), I 20,

4 Stitch three J wall sections to two K window sections in the

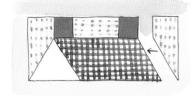

following order: wall/window/ wall/window/wall.

5 Next, add an M wall strip to

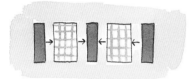

make the bottom of the school-house and an L wall strip above the windows to complete the house front.

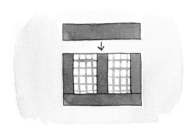

6 Join a side edging strip (N) to the front of the house and then stitch an O edging strip along the top edge.

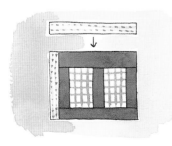

7 Make the side wall: stitch a G wall section to each side of a side window (H).

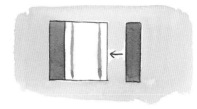

8 Add an I wall section to the bottom of the side section, and an F piece to the top.

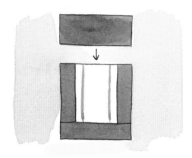

9 Stitch the side and front sections together to complete the main house.

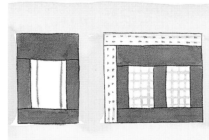

10 To finish the block, stitch the house to the roof and sky section. Make 19 more blocks in the same way.

11 Join the blocks together in rows, setting a Q sashing strip between each block to make four rows, each with five blocks and four sashing strips.

12 Join the rows together, setting a P sashing strip between each row.

13 Join the quilt back pieces together along one long edge and press the seam to one side.

14 Assemble the top, batting, and backing together, as directed on page 13.

FINISHING

15 Tie the quilt layers together at intervals of approximately 3 in, arranging the ties so that they suit the pattern of the blocks. For each tie, thread a chenille needle with a long piece of doubled unknotted crochet cotton. Starting from the top of the quilt, take the needle through all layers, leaving an end of about 1¼ in long on top. Take the needle back up, close to the first hole, and then down again. Now bring it back up a second time. Trim the thread to the same length as the loose end (about 1¼ in). Tie the ends together in a square knot (right over left, and then left over right), then trim them to an even 1 in.

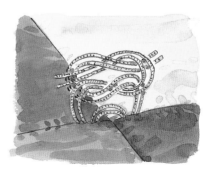

Roman Cross

Many patchwork tops, like this attractive example, were left unquilted, perhaps for use as summer bedcovers. Sometimes, in any case, not all the patchwork covers that a girl made for her hope chest would be quilted, a number being left unfinished for completion later. However, it would be a simple matter to turn this cover into a quilt: simply take a piece of batting the size of the finished cover and insert it between the two layers at the assembly stage in the usual way.

This particular block could easily be adapted to a Friendship quilt, in which each block is made and signed by a different person. The blocks are then joined together and the finished quilt presented as a going-away or wedding gift, or to mark some other special event. In this case, the central cross could be cut from white fabric, to take the embroidered signature.

The block itself is not complicated to make up, but seams must be matched carefully to achieve the attractive geometric effect.

Red and white was a common combination for patchwork tops, but there is no reason why you should restrict yourself to these colors. As with the Lady of the Lake design (page 52), this pattern looks attractive in many different color combinations. If you want to change the colors, first make a small-scale colored diagram on graph paper, or cut out small-scale patches from fabric samples. Glue them in the correct design order on a paper background for an accurate impression of what the quilt would look like in your chosen color combination.

ABILITY LEVEL:
Intermediate

SIZE OF FINISHED QUILT:
79 x 91 in

SIZE OF BLOCK:
8½ in square, 20 patchwork and 30 plain blocks required

MATERIALS:
- 1¾ yd colored print fabric
- 10½ yd white fabric (includes fabric for back of quilt)

- Templates for pieces A–I (template patterns are given on page 123, measurements do not include seam allowances).

RIGHT Made in England around the turn of the century, this Roman Cross design was stitched in the familiar red-and-white combination, but it could be made in colors chosen to suit your room setting with the proviso that the block demands a strong color contrast to make the most of the cross shape.

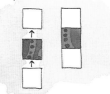

make two rectangles, each white/ colored/white.

2 Join the patchwork rectangles, one to each side of a colored C rectangle, making a square, press. Join a white C rectangle to each side of the pieced square.

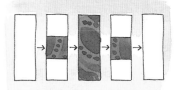

3 Take a white C rectangle, and join a colored D triangle to each short end; repeat, making a mirror-image, with the colored triangles facing the opposite way.

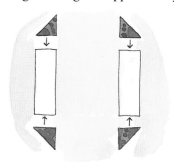

4 Join one of these strips to each side of the large pieced rectangle made in step 2.

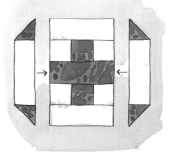

CUTTING

Note: a ¼ in seam allowance is included in all measurements. Pattern pieces do not include a seam allowance.

Back of quilt Two pieces, 40¼ x 91¾ in, white fabric

Plain blocks Thirty 9in squares (J), white fabric

Border Two pieces 10¼ x 72½ in, and two pieces 10¼ x 80 in, white fabric

Pattern pieces

Note: The number of pieces for a single block are shown in brackets. Pattern pieces are given on page 123.
Colored fabric: A 98 (4), B 58 (2), C 20 (1), D 360 (12), E 88, F 4, H 4, I 18
White fabric: B 218 (8), C 98 (4), F44, G44.

PIECING

1 With right sides together, join a white B square to a colored B square. Join a second white B square to the opposite side of the colored B square. Repeat to

5 Join a colored D triangle to each of two opposite sides of a white B square. Join a colored A triangle to one of the remaining sides. Repeat three more times.

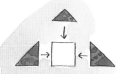

6 To complete the block, join the four corners to the central piece. Make 19 more identical blocks.

Half blocks
7 Join a white B square to a colored B square. Join a second white B square to the opposite side of the colored B square. Join to a colored I rectangle

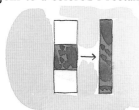

8 Join a white G piece to each end of the pieced rectangle.

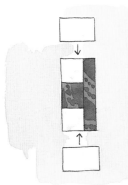

9 Join a D triangle to each end of a white C rectangle. Following step 5, make one corner piece. Join the two corner pieces together.

10 Join a white F piece to a colored D triangle, then add an E triangle. Repeat, this time making a mirror-image piece.

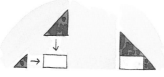

11 Join the four pieces together to complete the half block. Make 17 more identical half blocks.

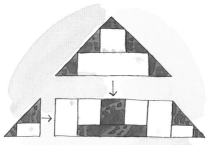

Quarter block
12 Join a colored F piece to a white B square, and join these to a colored H rectangle.

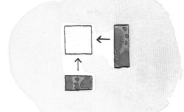

13 Join a white G piece to the pieced square. Take a second white G piece and join a colored D triangle to one end, making sure that it will face the correct way to be joined to the first G piece.

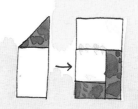

14 Following step 10, make two corners.

15 Join the four pieces to complete the quarter block. Make three more quarter blocks.

16 Sew the blocks together in diagonal rows, starting with the middle rows and working out to each corner, adding half or quarter blocks to each end.

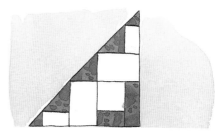

17 Matching seams, sew the rows together. To finish, add the two remaining quarter blocks.

18 Take the two shorter border strips, and add one to each long side of the patchwork. Add the remaining border strips to the top and bottom.

19 For the back, sew the two pieces together lengthwise. Press the seam allowances to one side.

20 Assemble the top and back together (see page 13).

FINISHING
21 Quilt lightly with zigzag lines set 1 in apart. The quilting lines stop 1 in in from the raw edges.

22 Turn in the edges and finish as directed for *Folded edges* on page 15.

Crown and Thorns

The strong, bold use of color contrasts in this striking design is typical of many quilts made by the Amish. The Amish are a Swiss-German Protestant sect, who first settled in Pennsylvania, in the United States, in the early 18th century. Their way of life is simple: ornamentation is frowned upon and clothing and furniture are kept plain.

Amish quilts are typically made from plain fabrics. Block patterns are often square in shape and large in scale. Generally, the more complicated block designs, as favored by the "English" (as all non-Amish are called), find little favor with the Amish; as with patterned fabrics, it is considered worldly and extravagant to have too many pieces in a quilt top.

In the 19th century, some Amish groups moved to the Midwest, and the quiltmakers in these communities were more influenced by their "English" neighbors. As a result, Iowa and Ohio Amish quilts are more often rectangular and the piecing can be more elaborate.

However, the bold use of color remained, as seen in this example, where the dark-green sets off the lighter blocks to perfection. The quilting here is detailed, and this again is typical of Amish quilts, in which the simple patterns are counterpoised by flowing quilting designs.

ABILITY LEVEL:

Intermediate

SIZE OF FINISHED QUILT:

93½ x 78½ in

SIZE OF BLOCK:

10½ in square, 32 blocks required (20 pieced and 12 plain)

MATERIALS:

- 8 yd dark-green fabric (includes fabric for back of quilt)
- 2⅛ yd) purple fabric (allow strips for inner border to be cut without piecing; for economy, use fabric 36in wide)
- 1¼ yd blue-gray fabric
- 24 in white fabric
- 12 in each of red, peach, black, and beige fabrics
- Small piece, 12 in square, lilac fabric
- 93½ x 78½ in piece of batting Templates for the following pieces (templates are on page 124, measurements do not include seam allowances):
A triangle
B small square

RIGHT Quilts made by the Amish communities of America are very much sought by collectors. This vibrant quilt, with its strong, varied quilting patterns and bold use of color, was made in Iowa in the 1920s.

Inner border Cut two pieces 4 x 75 in, and two pieces 4 x 67 in, purple fabric

Binding Cutting along the length of the blue-gray fabric, cut eight equal strips, each 1 in wide. Join these together to make one long strip, not less than 9⅔ yd in length (this includes some extra fabric for easing around corners).

Plain blocks Cut twelve 11 in squares, dark-green fabric

Side triangles Cut seven 11⅜ in squares, dark-green fabric. Cut each of these in half diagonally.

Corners Cut one 11⅞ in square, dark-green fabric. Cut diagonally to produce four quarters.

Pattern pieces
Blue-gray fabric: 224 A triangles, 56 B squares
White fabric: 160 A triangles, 50 B squares
Red fabric: 80 A triangles, 25 B squares
Peach fabric: 64 A triangles, 20 B squares
Black fabric: 48 A triangles, 12 B squares
Beige fabric: 48 A triangles, 12 B squares
Lilac fabric: 16 A triangles, 5 B squares

PIECING
1 Take a triangle of red fabric (background), and stitch it to a triangle of blue-gray fabric (crown and thorns) to make a square. Repeat 15 times, making a total of 16 red/blue-gray squares.

CUTTING
Note: a ¼ in seam allowance is included in all measurements. Pattern pieces do not include a seam allowance.

Back of quilt Cut two pieces, 93½ x 39¾ in, dark-green fabric

Outer border Cut two pieces 6¼ x 82 in, and two pieces 6½ x 78½ in, dark-green fabric

2 Take two pieced squares and join them to make a strip – red/blue-gray/red/blue-gray. Make a second strip the same, and then stitch the two together to make one corner of the block.

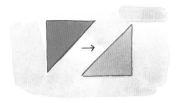

3 Repeat three times, taking care to alternate the colors.

4 Stitch a red square to a blue-gray square. Repeat to make two pairs of squares.

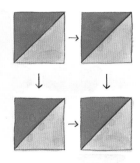

5 Stitch a corner section to one of the pairs of squares, and a second corner section to the other side, with blue triangles on the inside. Make a second piece in the same way.

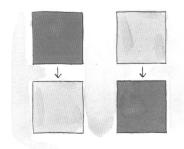

6 Stitch a row of squares in the following order – red/blue-gray/red/blue-gray/red.

7 Join the three sections together, making sure that there

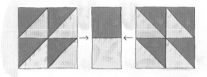

is a red (background) triangle at each corner.

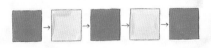

8 Make four more blocks with the same colors; then make three peach (background) and blue-gray (crown and thorns); one peach (background) and black (crown and thorns); six white (background) and blue-gray (crown and thorns); three white (background) and blue-gray (crown and thorns); one white (background) and blue-gray (crown and thorns); and one lilac (background) and black (crown and thorns) – 20 blocks in all.

9 Following the assembly diagram, join the blocks into diagonal rows, alternating patchwork blocks with plain ones, and starting and finishing with a triangle or corner piece, as appropriate.

10 Join the rows together to complete the middle of the patchwork.

11 Stitch the two longer purple border strips, one to each (long) side of the patchwork. Stitch the two shorter purple strips along the top and bottom to complete the inner border.

12 Stitch the two longer, dark-green outer border strips to the sides, and then the two shorter strips along the top and bottom, completing the quilt top.

13 For the back, sew the two lengths of dark-green fabric together, lengthwise. Press the seam allowance to one side.

14 Assemble the top, batting, and backing together, as directed on page 13.

FINISHING
15 Contour-quilt around the patches in the pieced blocks, as shown.

16 Next, quilt the edging and corner triangles with cross-hatched diagonal lines, set 2 in apart.

17 Quilt the plain, dark-green blocks with the flower pattern given on page 125, the purple border with the leaf pattern, and the dark-green border with the cable design.

18 Trim the edges to finish them, then attach the blue-gray binding, as described for a *Separate binding* on page 15.

Ice-Cream Parlor

The appearance of a quilt block can change dramatically according to the color combination used and the ways in which dark and light fabrics are set together. This is just one reason why the same block may have several different names. For example, a block that is commonly called Shoo Fly changes its name to Chinese Coin when it is made up of green and yellow combined with white.

Ice-Cream Parlor seems a particularly appropriate name for this quilt, with its cool, fresh pistachio, strawberry, and vanilla coloring, but the block used here is normally called either Goose in the Pond or Young Man's Fancy – perhaps, disappointingly, all the young man fancied was an ice cream!

The use of color here is very effective, and whatever fabrics are used, it would certainly be attractive to retain the stripes and checks of the central squares in some form or another.

This particular pattern, with its crisp, fresh appearance, is ideally suited to machine stitching. At any rate, the slightly softer effect of hand stitching would not necessarily add anything to the design. The quilting is simplicity itself – just diamond crosshatching – but you might choose to abandon this for an alternative quilting design. For example, you could complement machine patchwork by quilting "in the ditch" (i.e. along the seamlines), again by machine. The white squares could then be decorated with a hand-quilted motif, such as a rose, to provide a subtle contrast to the rest of the quilt.

ABILITY LEVEL:
Beginner/Intermediate

SIZE OF FINISHED QUILT:
70 x 87¼ in

SIZE OF BLOCK:
17¼ in, 20 blocks required

MATERIALS:
- 7¼ yd white fabric (includes fabric for back of quilt)
- Four fabrics for patchwork, as follows:
  1½ yd green patterned fabric
  1½ yd pink patterned fabric

  28 in green and white striped fabric
  28 in red checked fabric
- 71 x 88¼ in piece of batting

RIGHT Made around the turn of the 20th century, this quilt successfully combines cool, fresh greens with the warmth of pink and red, offset by white. The resulting design would give a light and airy feeling to any bedroom.

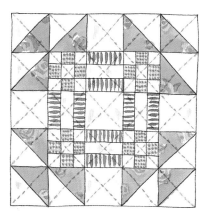

B: 100 (5) white 4 in squares
C: 160 (8) green stripe; 80 (4) white
D: 400 (20) white; 320 (16) red check

PREPARING PATTERN PIECES

1 From white, green, and pink fabrics, cut A triangles. The simplest way to do this is to mark 4⅜ in squares on the top fabric with a rotary cutter then to cut these diagonally in half to produce triangles.

2 Cutting across the width of the fabric (assuming the stripes run the length of the fabric), cut 1⅝ in strips: 16 from green stripe; 15 from red check, and 33 from white fabric.

3 Join strips along their length to make pieced strips as follows: 8 pieces, green striped/white/ green striped; 5 pieces red check/white/red check; and 10 pieces white/red check/white.

4 Cut across the pieced strips; cut green/white/green strips into 4 in squares, as shown.

CUTTING

Note: a ¼ in seam allowance is included in all measurements.

Back of quilt Two pieces, 74 x 44 in, white fabric

Pattern pieces
Number of pieces for a single block are in brackets; see steps 1-4 for how to prepare pieces A, C and D.
A: 240 (12) white; 120 (12) green pattern; 20 (12) pink pattern

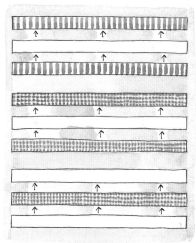

PIECING

5 Cut across red check/white/ red check to make 80 strips each 4 x 1⅝ in, and across the white/

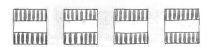

red/white to make 160 strips, also 4 x 1⅝ in.

Take one red check/white/red check strip and enclose it between two white/red check/white strips to make a square. Make sure that you take great care to match seamlines accurately. Make three more squares in the same manner.

6 Working along the long edge, join one white A triangle to a green patterned A triangle. Repeat to make 12 more identical white and green squares.

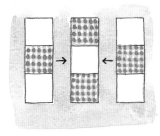

7 Taking care to angle the triangles correctly, join the patchwork squares into five rows.

8 Join the rows into the completed block, and then make 19 more blocks – a total

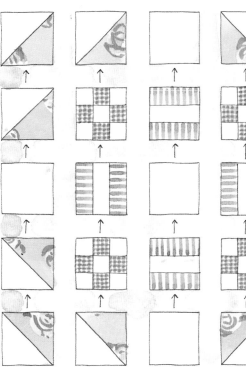

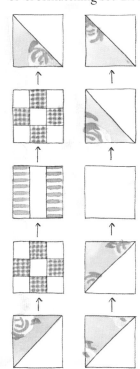

of 10 with green triangles and 10 with pink ones.

9 Join the blocks into four rows: two rows green/pink/green/ pink/green, and two rows pink/green/pink/green/ pink. Join the rows together to complete the quilt top.

10 For the quilt back, join the pieces along one long edge and press the seams to one side.

11 Assemble the quilt top, batting, and backing, as directed on page 13.

FINISHING

12 Quilt with diagonal rows of crosshatching set 2⅜ in apart.

13 Next, trim the batting to extend beyond the patchwork for an even ¼ in on all sides. Trim the backing to extend ¾ in beyond the batting. Turn under a ¼ in seam allowance on all sides of the backing and bring the folded edge over to the front, covering the edges of the patchwork for just ¼ in. Pin and baste. Fold neatly at the corners, and machine stitch in place, close to the folded edge.

Pillows and Cushions

Patchworks complement and enhance each other. A collection of patchwork pillows scattered over a bed or sofa creates a country-style effect and adds to the interest of other quilts and throws. Each of the designs shown here is easy and quick to make, and provides a good way of using up odd scraps of fabric.

The Single Irish Chain design makes an ideal partner for the Bordered Chain Quilt on page 64; the second design, Pinwheels, is found at the joining of Ocean Waves blocks (see page 47). To use this pattern for large pillows or cushions, it looks attractive if you alternate the pieced squares with plain ones. The large patchwork cushion is made simply by joining strips of patchwork; as with the Postage Stamp design on page 110, the patches can consist of random lengths, provided the width of the patches within each strip remains constant.

Only the Single Irish Chain pillow features quilting; Pinwheels and Simple Patchwork require no batting layer, although if they are to receive a lot of wear and tear, apply a backing layer along the seamlines.

ABILITY LEVEL:

Beginner

SIZE OF FINISHED COVERS:

Pinwheels – 9 in square

Single Irish Chain – 10½ in square

Simple Patchwork – 16 in square

MATERIALS:

Pinwheels

- Scraps (brushed cotton or wool /cotton mixture) for patchwork - two 3⅛ in squares contrasting fabrics for the pinwheels

- 10 in square, plain or patterned fabric for the back
- Pillow form

Single Irish Chain

- ⅓ yd white cotton fabric
- 8 in square, dark-blue cotton fabric
- 11 in square, thin batting
- 11 in square, lightweight cotton fabric (to back the batting layer for the quilting)
- Pillow form

Simple Patchwork

- Fabric scraps (see *Pinwheels*) for the patchwork – each large, plain square measures 4½ in square, the small squares are 2½ in, and a pair of triangles can be cut from a 4⅞ in square of fabric
- 17 in square of fabric for the back
- Pillow form

RIGHT A scattering of patchwork pillows – quick to make, even for complete beginners – lends a welcoming atmosphere to a room. Use colors that blend in with, but are not identical to, other textiles in the room.

Pinwheels

Single Irish Chain

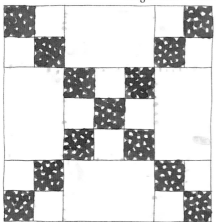

Simple Patchwork

CUTTING

Pinwheels For each of the four pinwheels, cut four 3⅛ in squares, two from each of the two fabrics. Cut each square in half diagonally. When you have finished, you will have a total of 32 triangles for all four pinwheels.

Single Irish Chain 11½ in square of white fabric for the back. For the patchwork, cut 2 in squares, 12 from white fabric and 13 from dark-blue. From white fabric, cut four rectangles, each 5 x 3½ in.

Simple Patchwork For each four-square patch (there are four in all), cut four 4½ in squares, two each from two contrasting fabrics; a total of 16 squares for the cover. Cut eight 4⅞ in squares of fabric and cut each diagonally, making 16 triangles. Cut four 4½ in squares for the large patches.

ASSEMBLY

Pinwheels

1 Take a total of eight triangles, four each from two fabrics. Join a pair of contrasting triangles. Repeat to make four squares

2 Join the four squares together,

making sure that you avoid joining sides of the same color.

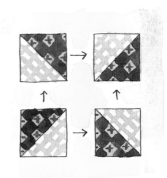

3 Make three more identical pinwheels in the same way. Join them two-by-two and then join the two pairs to complete the patchwork front.

Single Irish Chain

1 Stitch a white square to a dark-blue square. Repeat seven times to produce a total of eight two-square patches.

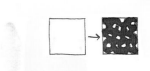

2 Stitch two of the two-square patches together, making a four-patch square. Repeat twice to make three more squares.

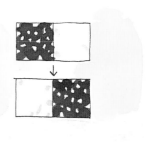

3 Take three square patches, two blue and one white, and stitch them together – blue/white/blue. Make a second strip the same. Take two white squares and one blue and join them – white/blue/white.

4 Join the three rows together to make the central square of the pillow cover.

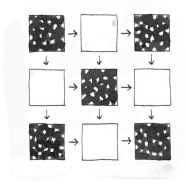

5 Following the diagram, join the cover into three rows: four-patch square/white rectangle/four-patch square; rectangle/nine-patch square/rectangle; and four-patch square/rectangle/four-patch square. Join the rows together to complete the patchwork.

6 The white rectangles are quilted in a simple pattern of your choice, such as the flower on page 124. First, assemble the three layers for the pillow front and baste in the same way as for a full-scale quilt.

7 Quilt the design on the white rectangles, and then contour-quilt around the inside of each small square.

Simple Patchwork

1 Take four small squares, two from each of two contrasting fabrics. Take a patch from each fabric and stitch them together. Repeat with the remaining two patches, and then join the two pairs together to make a four-patch square (see steps 1 and 2 for *Single Irish Chain*). Make three more four-patch squares.

2 Take two triangles from two contrasting fabrics and stitch the long edges together to form a square (as in step 1 of *Pinwheels*). Make seven more two-triangle squares in the same way.

3 Join the squares into rows: row 1, four-patch square/plain square/four-patch square/plain square; row 2, four two-triangle squares; row 3, plain square/four-patch square/plain square/four-patch square; and row 4, four two-triangle squares.

4 Stitch the four rows together to complete the patchwork.

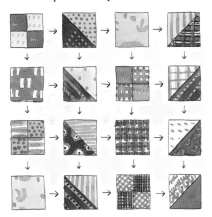

FINISHING
All covers

1 Take the piece of fabric for the pillow back and, with right sides together and raw edges even, pin and baste the pillow front and the pieces back together. The back of the pillow cover will measure approximately ¼ in larger all around than the front.

2 Taking a ½ in seam allowance on the fabric for the back, and ¼ in on the front (patchwork) side, machine stitch around all four edges of the pillow, leaving a gap in the middle of one side for inserting the filling. The gap should measure approximately 7¼ in long for the *Pinwheels* cover, 8¾ in long for the *Single Irish Chain* cover, and 12 in long for the *Simple Patchwork* cover.

3 Trim the seam allowance neatly across the four corners to reduce bulk, then turn the cover right side out. Press flat.

4 Finally, insert the pillow form and slipstitch the gap or insert a zipper.

Template-free Patchwork

Patchwork quiltmaking has changed dramatically since its inception, thanks to new cutting and sewing methods. Sewing machines, rotary cutters, and other labor saving devices have enabled many quiltmakers to concentrate on design, color choices, and the enjoyment of the creation of a quilt rather than the repetitive and time consuming preparations that were necessary in the past.

The most important tool in template-free patchwork is the rotary cutter, which enables the quiltmaker to cut through four layers of fabric at once - a great time saver, especially when hundreds of pieces are required. The tool is extremely accurate when used properly and will also speed up the sewing because the pieces fit together easily. It is used in conjunction with a self-healing mat and a thick plastic ruler manufactured especially for quiltmakers.

ABOVE AND RIGHT *Many simple patchwork shapes can easily be marked and cut with a quilter's ruler and a rotary cutter, without any requirement for templates. Neither the Postage Stamp above nor the Random Postage Stamp quilt on the right require templates, yet both are attractive, partly because of their pleasing combination of textile patterns and solid colors.*

Green and White Maze

The design of this quilt, with its bold geometric lines of white interspersed with cool-green triangles and squares, is utterly simple, but all the more striking and effective for that. The block itself is similar to one known as Mountain Peak, but the feeling here is not so much that of a mountain, as of a formal garden, with paths running off at angles and neat, low hedges. The sashing strips, often used to divide a quilt into individual, identifiable blocks, are here cleverly employed to link the blocks and are an integral part of the overall design.

This piece was never quilted, but was simply backed for use as a summer coverlet. It is not generally recommended to use quilts as covers for dining tables, as frequent washing pulls at the stitching and tends to make the middle layer shift and break up, but an unquilted coverlet, especially if it has been well made, should be able to take more washing than a quilt, and you can always protect it with a sheet of clear plastic during mealtimes.

Providing you are careful to link up the lines with geometrical precision, this makes a suitable project – straightforward, yet highly rewarding – for a newcomer to quiltmaking, especially if you make it into a coverlet, rather than a padded quilt. However, mistakes or inaccurate piecing show up very clearly in a bold pattern like this, so take care to pin pieces together accurately before stitching.

ABILITY LEVEL:
Beginner

SIZE OF FINISHED QUILT:
75¾ x 69¼ in

SIZE OF BLOCK:
11⅜ in square, 30 blocks required

MATERIALS:
• 6½ yd white fabric (includes fabric for patchwork and back of quilt)
• 2⅓ yd green print fabric
• 75¾ x 69¼ in piece of batting (optional – the original was left as a coverlet)
• Set square for marking edges (see steps)

RIGHT Made in England in the 1860s, this stylish quilt, with its refreshing combination of white and green, features a large, simple block that would be easy for a beginner to assemble.

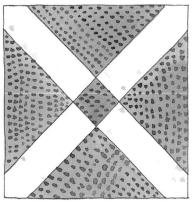

2½ in strips, white fabric, and 24 2½ in squares, green fabric (additional squares of this size are required for the Green Maze blocks, see *Pattern pieces,* below)

Pattern pieces
From green fabric, cut thirty 12⅝ in squares, and cut each one diagonally into four triangles. Also from green fabric, cut thirty 2½ in squares. From white fabric, cut 120 strips, each 2½ x 7¾ in.

PIECING
Green maze block
1 Take a green triangle and stitch it to a strip of white fabric. The right-angled point of the triangle should be joined to the strip so that a short side of the triangle and the short edge of the strip form a continuous line; at the other end, the strip extends slightly beyond the edge of the triangle.

2 Join a second triangle to the other side of the white strip. Press the seam allowance to the green side, then using a set square mark a right-angled corner on the

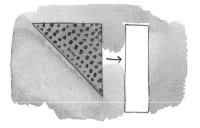

white strip. Trim to complete one corner of the block.

3 Make another (opposite) corner in the same way.

CUTTING
Note: a ¼ in seam is included in all measurements.

Back of quilt Two pieces, 31 x 70¼ in white fabric

Border Two pieces 3 x 64⅞ in, and two pieces 3 x 76¾ in, white fabric

Sashing strips Forty-nine 11⅞ x

4 Take two white strips and a green square. Stitch the strips to opposite sides of the green square.

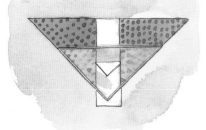

5 Join the two corner sections, one to each side of the white/green/white strip. The white strips at the middle of each corner section should line

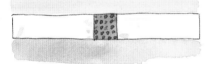

up with the two remaining sides of the green square.

6 Again using the set square, mark and trim the two ends of the middle strip, making right-angled corners, as before.

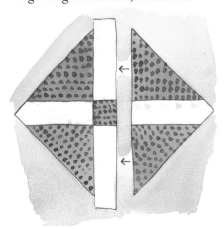

7 Make 29 more blocks in the same way.

8 Prepare the horizontal sashing strips as follows: take five white strips and four green squares. Stitch them together to make one long strip, white/green/white/green/white/green/white/green/white. Make four more identical sashing strips in the same way.

9 Join the Green Maze blocks into rows of five blocks, each separated by one white sashing strip.

10 Alternating rows of blocks with the prepared sashing strips, join the rows together to complete the pieced top.

11 Take the two short border strips and stitch them to the top and bottom of the quilt, then stitch the two longer strips down the sides.

12 For the back, sew the two pieces of white fabric together along the long edge. Press the seam to one side.

13 Assemble the top and back together (see page 13), adding a batting layer in between if desired. If you decide to add a layer of batting, you will find that the quilt back and front extend beyond this layer for ½ in all around.

FINISHING
14 As this coverlet did not have a middle layer to be held in position, the quilting was minimal – just contour quilting around the squares and the triangles of the blocks.

15 If you decide to add a layer of batting, you will need to quilt more closely. For example, you

might make crosshatched lines, set ¾ in apart, on the green triangles; alternatively, you could quilt along the sashing strips and the white strips of the blocks with a trailing leaf pattern (see page 126, and put a flower (see page 125) in the middle of each green square. The border quilting might have a similar floral theme.

16 To finish the coverlet, follow the directions *Folded edges,* given on page 15.

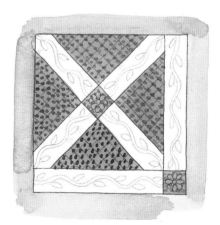

Strippy

Characteristic of the northeast of England, the Strippy quilt was produced by women who prided themselves on their quilting skills. Many of the North Country quilts were wholecloth, decorated with the highly elaborate quilting designs for which the region was famous. The Strippy was an economical and convenient patchwork variant, which allowed the quilting to predominate.

Most Strippies were in two contrasting colors, often red and white. Another tradition was to have a slightly different band, perhaps pieced, at the middle. The beauty of this particular quilt lies in the delicate lilac print used for the colored stripes, and the twisting leaf, vine, and flower design of the quilting.

It is unlikely that you will be able to find an identical fabric to the original, but you may find a cotton lawn that echoes the original print. This Strippy is included primarily as a type of quilt – one which makes an excellent starter project, and which you should adapt at will.

You can join the pieces and then assemble the layers, and quilt in the normal fashion. Alternatively, you might prefer the quilt-as-you-go technique described here. This is a good way of practicing different quilting patterns without having to work a full-scale unified design.

ABILITY LEVEL:
Beginner (quilt-as-you-go), or Intermediate (if using the quilting pattern as described in step 4, on page 98)

SIZE OF FINISHED QUILT:
88 x 84 in

SIZE OF STRIP:
8 in wide, 11 strips

MATERIALS:
- 8 yd white fabric includes fabric for backing)

- Printed or plain fabric for colored strips; these may be the same, or varied patterns You will need enough for six strips. If you are using the traditional method (see step 2) the four middle strips will be 8½ x 85 in, and the two outer strips 8¾ x 85 in. For the quilt-as-you-go technique, the strip widths should be 9 in (four strips) and 9¼ in (two strips).

- The traditional method needs 88 x 84 in of batting. If using the-quilt-as-you-go technique, you need 95 x 84in of batting. A thin filling was used for the original quilt, which made it easier to quilt the details of the pattern.

RIGHT The elaborate floral quilting design on this English strippy suggests that unlike the majority of strippies, this quilt may have come from the West Country.

the arrangement, cut your full-size strips.

Traditional sewing method: cut five white and four print strips, each 8½ x 85 in, and two (outside edge) print strips, each 8¾ x 85 in (this includes the seam allowance for the sides of the quilt).

Quilt-as-you-go method: (see step 6 onward) cut five white and four print strips 9 x 85 in, and two (outside edge) print strips each 9¼ x 85 in wide.

Traditional sewing method
3 Join the strips. The wider (print) strips are on the two outside edges, and print and white strips alternate. If you are machine-stitching, sew the seams alternately, first from top to bottom, and then from bottom to top – this will help to even out any stretching. Working from the middle out, join two large sections, then join the sections. Press seams to one side.

4 Mark and quilt your chosen pattern, making sure that all quilting lines stop 1 in clear of the raw edges to allow for hems. The quilting pattern of the original is a large-scale design featuring an elaborate display of grapes, vine leaves, and trailing stems. The original quilting lines run across the seamlines. It is repeated six times, with two rows of three repeats, the upper row being reversed to face the opposite way from the lower row. You could simplify the original quilting pattern (above, left),

CUTTING
Back of quilt For the traditional sewing method, cut two pieces, 44¾ x 85 in, white fabric. For the quilt-as-you-go method, cut a strip of white fabric to the same size as each strip cut for the quilt top (see step 2).

Fabric strips Depends on your sewing method (see step 2).

Batting For the quilt-as-you-go method, cut eleven 8½ x 84 in strips of batting.

PIECING
1 If you are using a variety of fabrics, rather than two, decide in what order to arrange the strips; whether you will have any repeat strips; which strips will be composed of several fabrics, and so on. You may find it helpful to make a small-scale plan by gluing miniature strips to paper in your chosen order.

Also plan your quilting pattern. You may decide to copy the naturalistic pattern of the original, or you may experiment with a range of patterns, particularly if you are using the quilt-as-you-go method.

2 When you are satisfied with

drawing it freehand on a sheet of paper to achieve a free-flowing effect. Then scale your pattern up to its full size and transfer it to the quilt with dressmaker's carbon paper.

5 For the back, join the two pieces together along the long edge. Press the seam to one side.

6 Assemble the marked quilt top, batting, and backing as directed on page 13.

7 Quilt the marked design, then proceed to step 15.

Quilt-as-you-go method
8 Mark your chosen quilting pattern on a strip of top fabric. You can use elements from this pattern, but redraw the stems to confine the pattern within the limits of a strip. When marking the pattern, start by basting a central, horizontal line across the width of the strip, and mark outward from this point to each end, so that the pattern runs symmetrically along the length.

9 Assemble the marked strip with a strip of batting and a backing strip of the same size as the marked strip. (If you are quilting a side strip first, it is important that the top and backing fabric extend beyond the batting for ¼ in more on the long side that will form a side of the quilt; in all other cases, center the batting on the backing strip when assembling layers). Baste the layers together (see page 13).

10 Quilt, taking care not to

allow any quilting lines to run into the seam allowance. Repeat until you have quilted each strip.

11 Lay the quilted strips out flat and work out a practical joining sequence; for example, into pairs and then larger units. Take the first pair of strips to be joined, fold back the batting and backing layers and, with right sides together, stitch the quilt top layer only along the length, taking a ½ in seam allowance. Trim, then press.

12 Open the two strips flat and

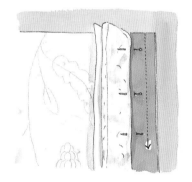

trim any surplus batting until the edges butt up against each other. Stitch the edges together, using either feather or herringbone stitch (see page 37).

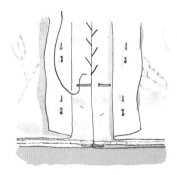

13 Bring one edge of the backing fabric over the joined batting layer; turn the other edge under and hand stitch, using either a matching thread and a blind stitch, or a decorative feather stitch and a contrasting thread.

14 Join all strips together in this way to complete the top.

FINISHING
15 If necessary, trim the batting to measure 88 x 84 in. Quilt a line around the outer edge, set ½ in in from the edge of the batting. Trim the top and backing to within 1 in of the quilted line.

16 Fold in the top and backing, so the folded edge is ½ in clear of the quilting. Pin and then stitch around the edge using either a double or single row of machine- or hand-stitching.

Welsh Wool Quilt

Quiltmaking has a strong tradition in Wales, for the same reasons of basic necessity, economy, and warmth as applied in the Midwest of the United States. However, unlike the American examples, many Welsh quilts were made from wool fabrics. The patches were sometimes taken from old clothing, but were often bought from textile mills in bundles when the manufacturer wanted to sell off old lines or sample books.

This particular quilt shows little wear in the patches, so it was probably made from mill bundles. The effect may be somewhat somber at first. Welsh textile mills predominantly made men's suiting, rather than women's dress fabrics, and the serious gray and brown tweeds and pin-striped wool and worsteds of this quilt evoke an era when most British men wore suits (rather than today's jeans).

This quilt is not beautiful in the conventional sense, and it is certainly not feminine, but it has a charm as solid and reliable as the smell of new-baked bread.

The quilt could be varied in many ways. You might use a thicker batting than usual and tie the patches at the corners, as for the quilt on page 32. Made in this way, perhaps with a few random patches cut from more brightly colored fabrics, it would make a cozy hearth rug for a weekend cabin.

ABILITY LEVEL:

Beginner

SIZE OF FINISHED QUILT:

71 x 43 in

MATERIALS:

- 2 yd brown or dark grey wool fabric, 60 in wide, for the quilt backing
- Scraps of tweed, wool or worsted fabrics, for the patchwork. 160 patches are needed and a 8⅜ in square of fabric will make two patches. The placement of patches on the original quilt is random; the maker alternated a dark gray (almost black with dark brown for the patches around much of the outer border, but clearly did not have enough fabric to maintain this sequence. The design in the middle is even more random, although, on the whole, brown and grey alternate, as do dark and light patches. For estimating fabric requirements, see below.
- 7⅓ yd black braid, 1 in wide, for binding
- 71 x 43 in piece of batting

RIGHT Wales, with its hills and sheep farms, has long been a center of the wool trade, and Welsh quilts, such as this one which was made in the 1880s, were traditionally made with wool rather than cotton fabrics.

ESTIMATING

This is very much a scrapbag project. The quilt shows little wear and was almost certainly made from new fabrics. It is not generally advisable to use fabrics taken from old clothing for quilts, but it might be possible in this instance, provided the clothes are not worn-out. For example, patches could be cut from a little-worn suit or jacket

that had been rejected for reasons of fashion rather than wear.

Wool fabrics vary considerably in width and are expensive, so estimate how much you need before buying. To do this, make a paper pattern or template of the shape required. In this instance, the patches are cut from a simple square, but the principle is the same for more complex quilts.

Take a piece of paper the width of your chosen fabric; the ideal paper to use is brown wrapping paper, which is inexpensive, and you can cut a piece easily to whatever fabric width you require.

Use your paper pattern or template(s) to draw outlines on the paper to see how many patches will fit across the fabric width. In this case, the size specified for the squares from which patches are cut includes the seam allowance, but in many cases you must leave two seam allowances between patches. Bearing this in mind, draw as many patches as you can across the marked fabric width. (With more complicated shapes, such as hexagons, which dovetail into each other, you may need to draw several rows in order to judge how many patches you will be able to cut from a given length and width of fabric.)

To estimate the length of fabric you will require, divide the total number of patches required by the number that will fit across the width of the fabric. Multiply this by the depth of each patch and you have the fabric length required.

For example, if you want to alternate brown or gray with black around the border of this quilt, you will require 32 black triangles cut from 16 black squares. Each square measures 8⅜ in, and you can fit seven squares across a fabric width of 60 in, five into a width of 45 in, and four into a 36 in width:

16/7 = 2 with 2 over, so a depth of 3 rows is required

8⅜ in = 25⅛ in of fabric, 60 in wide

CUTTING

Note: a ½ in seam allowance is included in all measurements instead of the usual ¼ in.

Back of quilt
From an assortment of fabrics,

cut eighty 8⅜ in squares. Cut each square diagonally in half to make a total of 160 triangular patches.

PIECING

1 If you are using a wide variety of fabrics, start by making a colored or number-coded assembly diagram on graph paper, showing the order that you are going to join the patches together. For greater speed, lay a piece of tracing paper over the assembly diagram shown here and, using a letter or number for each fabric, indicate the order of piecing.

2 When you are happy with the arrangement, join the first pair of patches along the long sides. Remember to take a ½ in seam allowance throughout.

3 Working from the bottom of

the quilt upward, join all the pairs of patches in the bottom row, making eight squares. Stitch the squares together to make a long strip, see below.

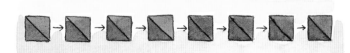

4 Repeat until you have completed all the rows.

5 Stitch the rows together; start by joining the two top rows, then the two bottom rows, add more rows and finally join the two halves of the top together.

6 Assemble the top, batting and backing (see page 13)

7 Quilt with lines of cross-hatching, running diagonally across the quilt. The lines of the original are 3 in apart.

8 Trim the four edges of the quilt to even them. Fold the braid over the raw edges of the quilt, making mitered tucks at the corners, and turning under the raw overlapping edge of braid at the point where the two edges meet (start and finish about a third of the way along a side edge). Pin and baste the braid in position, then machine stitch it in place, stitching through all layers.

If your machine cannot cope with this thickness, you may have to attach the braid by hand, or machine stitch it in place around the top; fold it over to the back of the quilt, and handstitch at the back.

Medallion

The medallion is a category of quilt embracing a range of design types. Virtually any quilt that consists of borders surrounding a strong central image can be called a medallion design. The middle of the quilt may be a large fabric shape, a patchwork image, an appliqué design, or even embroidery.

The borders can take the form of straight strips of fabric, with squares at the corners, as with the larger quilt featured here, or they may incorporate pieced designs. If the borders are patchwork, it is usual to have a different patchwork pattern for each separate border. The number of borders varies, but there are always at least two, and they generally increase in size toward the edge of the quilt.

Early medallion quilts were the preserve of wealthy and fashionable households. In the 17th century, motifs from exotic Indian chintz fabrics were cut out and applied to quilts with the technique known as broderie perse, often within medallion designs.

At the other end of the spectrum are the medallion quilts produced by Amish women. These dramatic quilts are restricted to a strong central image and surrounded by one plain border. The fabrics are solid cottons, although the quilting patterns are often elaborate.

The two medallion quilts shown here provide an introduction to this type of design, but you may choose to vary them, perhaps by adding patchwork borders taken from other quilts.

ABILITY LEVEL:
Beginner
SIZE OF FINISHED QUILT:
80 x 84 in
MATERIALS:
- Fabric as follows (original fabrics in parentheses): 23 x 25 in fabric A (chintz-type fabric); ¾ yd fabric B (yellow); 14 in square fabric C (brown/blue); ¾ yd fabric D (dark-brown, orange and beige floral); 1⅓ yd fabric E (pale-blue floral); 13in square fabric F (brown floral); 12⅔ yd fabric G (orange and brown floral); 2 yd fabric H (pink and red); 15 x 12 in fabric I (pale-blue and beige)
- 4½ yd white fabric for back of quilt
- 1yd fabric for binding
- 80 x 84 in piece of batting

RIGHT This turn-of-the-century English medallion quilt is unusual in being rectangular, albeit only just. Most medallion patterns are square, the central image being surrounded by borders of identical width. However, here the maker made her central panel slightly longer, in order to show a whole motif, then adjusted the width of the side borders to offset this effect.

Fabric H: cut two pieces 70 x 6½ in; and two pieces 69 x 8 in. Fabric I: cut in half each way to make four pieces, each 8 x 6½in.

PIECING

1 The seam allowance is ½ in throughout.

This quilt is very simple to make and is therefore an ideal project for a beginner to patchwork. If you have not used a sewing machine a great deal, you may have difficulty keeping your seams absolutely straight on long runs of this type. Always start by pinning very carefully – it is best to begin at the middle and the outer corners; then the middle points between pins; and then pin at intervals of about ½ in. Make sure that you place the pins at right angles to the edge of the fabric. In this way, the sewing-machine needle will pass over the pins easily without catching.

When machine-stitching, keep a steady pace, feeding the fabric through smoothly. The temptation is to stop and start, checking that you are sewing in a straight line, but this will cause the fabric to move slightly while you are checking and may result in a puckered seam.

2 Stitch the two 57.4 cm/23 in long strips of fabric B to the short edges (top and bottom) of fabric A. Join a square of fabric C to each end of each of the 62.5 cm/25 in strips of fabric B, and stitch these to each side of the central piece (A).

CUTTING

Note: as the pieces for this quilt are so large, there is no need to use narrow seams, so for added strength a ½ in seam allowance is included in all measurements.

Back of quilt Two pieces, 200 x 80 x 42½ in, white fabric

Binding Cut 10 strips, each 3 in wide across the full width (45 in) of the co-ordinating fabric. Stitch strips together so that the binding measures 11 yd approximately.

Pattern pieces
Fabric B: cut two pieces 23 x 7 in; two pieces 25 x 7 in; four 6½ in squares; and four pieces 7½ x 6 in.
Fabric C: cut in half each way to make four 7 in squares. Fabric D: cut two pieces 35 x 6½ in; and two pieces 37 x 7½ in.
Fabric E: cut two pieces 46 x 6½ in, and two pieces 48 x 6½ in. Fabric F: cut in half each way to make four 6½ in squares.
Fabric G: cut two pieces 57 x 6 in; and two pieces 59 x 7½ in.

3 In the same way, stitch the two 87.5 cm/35 in strips of fabric D to the top and bottom of the patchwork. Stitch a 6½ in square of fabric B to each end of each of the 37 in strips of fabric D. Stitch these to each side of the patchwork.

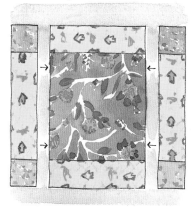

4 Stitch 46 in strips of fabric E to the top and bottom of the patchwork. Stitch a square of fabric F to each end of each of the 48 in strips of fabric E, and stitch these to each side of the patchwork.

5 Stitch 57 in strips of fabric G to the top and bottom of the patchwork. Stitch an 7½ x 6 in piece of fabric B to each end of each of the 59 in strips of fabric G and stitch these to each side of the patchwork.

6 Stitch 70 in strips of fabric H to the top and bottom of the patchwork. Next, stitch a 8 x 6½ in piece of fabric I one on each end of each of the 69 in strips of fabric H. Stitch the resulting strips to each side of the patchwork.

7 Join the two pieces of white backing fabric at the long edge, and press the seam to one side.

8 Assemble the top, batting, and backing together as directed on page 13.

FINISHING

9 The central rectangle is quilted in a pattern of overlapping circles known as Wineglass filling. To create this flower-like effect, you will need to use a circular template (here 2½ in in diameter) with notches at the four quarter points, to enable you to overlap the circles accurately.

10 The yellow border (fabric B) is quilted with lines of cross-hatching, set 2 in apart, which echo the angular geometric pattern.

11 Other borders, including the brown and orange fabric (D) and the pink with red trails (H) are quilted by following the trailing stems of the pattern. In a quilt

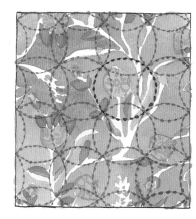

of this nature, where the emphasis is on the beauty of the fabrics used, this style of quilting helps to draw attention to the printed patterns.

12 Finish by stitching the binding around the edge, as directed on page 15 for *Separate binding.* Stitch it to the top first, taking a ¼ in seam allowance for the binding and a 1 in seam allowance for the quilt. Start at the middle of one side, and miter the binding at the corners, carefully folding

the binding and stitching the fold at an angle at the front and back of the quilt.

Small Medallion

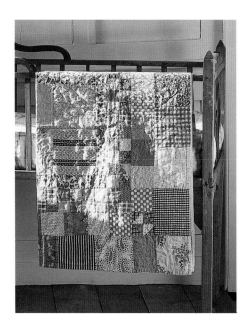

ABILITY LEVEL:
Beginner

SIZE OF FINISHED QUILT:
35 x 39½ in

MATERIALS:
• Assorted pastel fabrics. For the
middle, you need 6 in
squares in four different
printed fabrics. For more
details, see the *Cutting*
instructions below.

• 1⅓ yd of plain fabric, white or
lavender, for the back

CUTTING
Note: a ¼ in seam allowance is
included in all measurements.

Back of quilt 35 x 40½ in,
cotton fabric

Pattern pieces
Middle Four 6 in squares, each
from a different fabric

Border 1 Two pieces 12 x 2 in;
two pieces 14.5 x 2 in, all from
one fabric

Border 2 Thirty-six 2 in squares
(including four corner patches
from one fabric); eight 2 x 1½ in
patches

Border 3 Forty-four 2 in squares
(including four corner patches
from one fabric); eight 2 x 1½ in
patches

Border 4 Twenty-four 3½ in
squares and four 4½ x 2½ in
patches, from assorted fabrics.
For the corners, sixteen 2⅜ in
squares – eight from checked,
four from dark, and four from
light fabric. Cut each 2⅜ in
square in half diagonally, making
32 triangles.

Border 5 Fourteen 5¼ x 5 in
patches (including two corner
patches from one fabric), two
5¼ in squares (for top corners,
from the same fabric as the
other corners), six 5¼ x 3½ in
patches, three 5 x 2½ in patches,
four 5 in squares, two 5 x 3½ in
patches, and one 5 x 2½ in patch

Bottom row of quilt Two
5¼ in squares (for corners), four
5¼ x 5 in patches, two 13.1 x
5¼ x 3½ in patches and one 5 x
2½ in patch

PIECING
1 Stitch the four middle squares
together.

2 Stitch the two 12 x 2 in strips

*ABOVE Soft pastel prints, predominantly lilac in tone, make a charming cot cover. An extra row of squares at the bottom
converts it from a square into a rectangular cot quilt shape. Simple to make, this would make a delightful christening gift.*

to opposite sides of the four-square patch. Stitch the two 14.5 x 2 in strips to the two remaining sides (top and bottom).

3 Make border 2 rows: setting aside the corner patches, join together eight 2 in squares in a row, then add a 2 x 1½ in patch to each end of the strip. Repeat three times to make a total of four strips. Take two strips and add the four corner patches, one to each end of a strip.

4 Attach border 2 to the patchwork, sewing the short strips to opposite (top and bottom) sides first, and then adding the long strips.

5 Make border 3 rows: setting aside the corner patches, join 2 in squares in a row, then add a 2 x 1½ in patch to each end of the strip. Repeat three times to make a total of four strips. Take two strips and add the four corner patches, one to each end of a strip. Attach the border in the same way as described for border 2.

6 For border 4, start by making the corner sections. First, take one from the 16 triangles cut from check fabric and join it to one of the remaining 16 check triangles, making a square. Repeat 15 times to make 16 squares.

7 Arranging the fabrics as shown, so that the check fabric triangles are on the outside, stitch two squares together. Join

two more, and then join both pieces to make a large square,

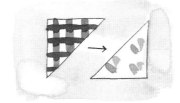

with the check fabrics on the outside and the other two fabrics alternating at the middle. Make three more corners in the same way.

8 Stitch three 3½ in squares in a row. Add an 4½ x 2½ in patch, then join three more 3½ in squares. Repeat three times to make four strips. Take two

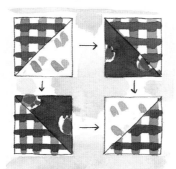

strips, and add a prepared corner block to each end of each strip. Join the short strips to the patchwork, and then the strips with corner blocks attached, as for the previous borders.

9 For border 5, setting aside the corner patches, join a 5¼ x 3½ in patch to two 5¼ x 5 in patches. Add a 5¼ x 2½ in patch; join this to a further two 5¼ x 5 in patches, and finish with a 5¼ x 3½ in patch. Repeat two more times to make three strips. Add the two 5¼ in, square corner

patches, one to each end of one of the strips (now the top row).

10 For the bottom row of border 5, make a strip as follows: one 5¼ x 5 in corner patch, one 5 x 3½ in patch (any fabric), two 5 in squares, a 5 x 2½ in patch, two 5 in squares, a 5 x 3½ in patch, and the remaining corner patch.

11 Make the bottom row as described in step 9, border 5, adding corner patches to each end. Stitch it to the rest of the patchwork.

FINISHING
12 The cover is quilted with a simple pattern of zigzag lines, set 1½ in apart. Leave 1 in clear around the unfinished edges of the cover.

13 Turn in the edges and finish as directed for *Folded edges* on page 15.

Postage Stamp

Order struggles against chaos in this charming but highly eccentric quilt. Essentially, the postage stamp pattern is one in which the patches in successive rows are of varying lengths, but all of the same width, adjustments being made to ensure that rows finish up the same length. However, in this quilt, the rows are organized around a central rectangle, and the corner patches are the same within each border. To achieve this regularity, the maker, or makers, cut some patches much smaller than others as they approached corners. The result is a jumbled confusion. The outer border strips also vary, being wider and more numerous on one side than the other. To simplify the pattern it has been regularized, but if you should wish to create a more random appearance, you could easily change the width of some border strips, and cut some patches longer than others.

The beauty of this quilt lies in its successful use of color and pattern. The strong red patch at the middle is echoed by red squares in the outer patchwork borders, and each patchwork border is restricted to fabrics of a similar tonal value and pattern type. The yellow and pink border strips provide an element of surprise and give the pattern movement. You will not be able to find identical prints and colors, but by retaining the contrast between subtle, neutral prints and strong, vibrant colors, you can recreate the liveliness of the original.

ABILITY LEVEL:

Intermediate

MATERIALS:

- 5⅓ yd white fabric (for back of quilt)
- Fabrics for patchwork, as follows:
  10 in red fabric (middle and borders 3 and 11)
  4 in dark-blue fabric (for borders 1, 6 and 11)
  4 in sea-green fabric (border 9)
  4 in dark-green fabric (borders 4 and 13)
  4 in yellow fabric (border 10)
  8 in deep-pink fabric (border 14)
  8 in pink printed fabric (border 14)
- Assortment of scrap fabrics for borders (1–9, 11 and 13). Each border must be distinct from adjacent borders, so assign batches of fabric to particular borders.
- For borders 15–21, see cutting instructions for actual sizes of strips.

LEFT The Postage Stamp design offers an excellent way of using up scraps of a wide variety of fabrics, as can be seen from this eccentric but attractive 19th-century English quilt.

111

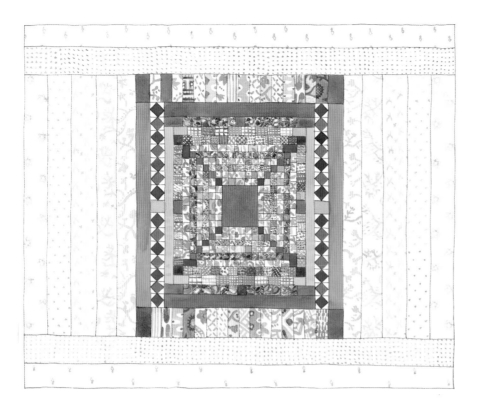

CUTTING

Note: a ¼ in seam allowance is included in all measurements.

Back of quilt Two pieces, 39¾ x 97 in, white fabric

Front of quilt
Middle 9 x 8½ in, red fabric
Border 1 Twenty 2 in squares (16 print fabrics, four blue fabric), two 2 x 3 in patches and two 2 x 2½ in patches, harmonizing print fabrics
Border 2 Twenty-eight 2 in squares (24 print fabrics, four pink fabric), two 2 x 3 in patches and two 2 x 2½ in patches, harmonizing print fabrics
Border 3 Thirty-six 2 in squares (32 print fabrics, four plain or

print red fabrics), two 2 x 3 in patches and two 2 x 2½ in patches, harmonizing print fabrics
Border 4 Forty-four 2 in squares (40 print fabrics, four dark-green fabric), two 2 x 3 in patches and two 2 x 2½ in patches, harmonizing fabrics
Border 5 Fifty-two 2 in squares (48 print fabrics, four plain purple fabrics), two 2 x 3 in patches and two 2 x 2½ in patches, harmonizing print fabrics
Border 6 Forty-two 2 x 2½ in patches and two 2 in squares, print fabrics, and four 2 x 3½ in patches, dark-blue fabric
Border 7 Fifty-four 2½ in squares (50 print fabrics, four brown fabric), and two 2½ x 3 in

patches, print fabrics
Border 8 Twenty 2½ x 3½ in patches, 16 harmonizing fabrics and four brown fabric
Border 9 Twenty-six 2½ in (24 harmonizing fabrics, two sea-green fabric), and four 4½ x 2½ in patches, sea-green fabric
Border 10 Two 35 x 2½ in strips, yellow fabric
Border 11 Twenty-eight 2⅝ in) squares (16 dark blue and 12 red), two 3½ x 3 in patches (contrast color), and fifty-six 2⅜ in squares (white fabric), cut all white squares diagonally in half to make 112 triangles
Border 12 Two 34½ x 3½ in strips, brown fabric
Border 13 Thirty-two 6½ x 3 in patches (harmonizing fabrics), and four 6½ x 3½ in patches, dark-green fabric
Border 14 Two 45 x 3½ in strips, pink fabric
Border 15 Two 57 x 4½ in strips, pink print fabric
Border 16 Two 57 x 4½ in strips, green print fabric
Border 17 Two 57 x 4½ in strips, pink print fabric
Border 16 Two 57 x 4½ in strips, green print fabric
Border 17 Two 57 x 6 in strips, beige/grey print fabric
Border 18 Two 57 x 6 in strips, beige fabric
Border 19 Two 57 x 6¾ in strips, green fabric
Border 20 Two 97 x 6½ in strips, blue print fabric
Border 21 Two strips, 97 x 5¾ in strips, green print fabric

PIECING

1 The simplest way to make this quilt is to cut, assemble, and attach each border successively, working from the middle out. Starting with border 1, stitch two small patches of harmonizing fabrics together. Repeat seven more times.

2 Attach a dark-blue patch to one end of a pair, repeat three more times. Join two strips into a row, setting a dark-blue patch at each end and adding a 2 x 3 in patch at the middle. Repeat, joining two more strips to make a second row.

3 Join two of the remaining pairs of patches into a third row, this time with a 2 x 2½ in patch at the middle. Repeat, making a fourth row.

4 Stitch a short row to each long side of the red middle. Stitch the two longer rows to the top and bottom. Repeat for borders 2–5.

5 For border 6 make two rows, each with five 2 x 2½ in patches, one 2 in square, five 2 x 2½ in patches, and one long dark blue patch. Join two rows of eleven 2 x 2½ in patches, and one long dark-blue patch. Attach the rows clockwise, piecing in the blue corner patch of the final row.

6 Make border 7 and attach it in

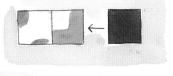

the same way as borders 1–5. Attach borders 8, 10, 9 and 12, in that order.

7 To make border 11, attach a

white triangle to each side of a square. Join the squares into two rows, with a contrast patch in the middle of each, as shown in

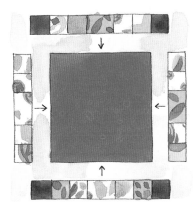

the assembly diagram.

8 Attach the two rows of border 11, then a border 14 strip to each side. Make up the two rows of border 13, with a dark-green patch at each end. Attach them to the top and bottom, then attach the side borders.

9 Finish by attaching the top and bottom border strips.

10 Sew the two pieces together along the long edge and press seams to one side.

11 Assemble the quilt top, batting and back as directed on page 13.

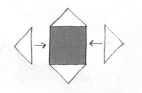

FINISHING
12 Quilt a line around the edge, 1 in in from the edge of the top. Quilt zigzag lines, set 1 in apart, stopping at the outer quilted line.

13 Trim the batting to measure ½ in less than the top and backing, then finish as for *Folded edges* on page 15.

Trip Around the World

The alternative name for this pattern is Granny's Dream. The two together conjure up an attractive picture of a globe-trotting old lady, intent on seeing the world.

With its ever-increasing rows of tiny patches, this pattern can easily look haphazard and rather bland, but colors are used to great effect in this particular quilt, giving it interest and movement. The violet and deep blue both contain and contrast with the many shades of yellow used. The warm yellows and pinks advance to meet the eye, standing out against the more neutral checks and white, while the cool green and stark white of the middle is unexpected and refreshing. Stronger, darker shades at the border help to frame the design, and the overall effect is beautifully harmonious and lively.

The basic pattern builds up into a square, but the maker of this quilt wanted a wide shape, so extra rows were added to the sides. These could be omitted, or further rows could be added, as desired. Most people making this style of quilt tend to use a mixture of scrapbag fabrics and freshly purchased materials. It pays to make a careful plan before you start, working out which fabrics to use for which rows, to avoid overspending.

ABILITY LEVEL:

Intermediate

SIZE OF FINISHED QUILT:

76½ x 71 in

MATERIALS:

- 4¾ yd white fabric (includes fabric for back of quilt)
- Small quantities of a total of 24 (including plain white) fabrics are required for patchwork: a 4 in strip of 45 in wide fabric will be adequate for a complete round of patches in one color from the central patch out for the first 18 rounds, but you will need slightly more if a fabric is to be used for several rounds, or for outer rounds.
- 76½ x 71 in piece of batting

RIGHT Plain shades and small-scale patterned fabrics (large patterns would have been disjointed by the small size of the patches) are successfully combined in this 1930s English quilt.

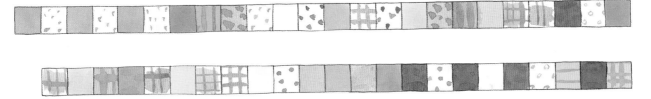

CUTTING

Note: a ¼ in seam allowance is included in all measurements.

Back of quilt Two pieces 76½ x 35¾ in, white fabric

Border Two pieces 4¾ x 73 in, and two pieces 2¾ x 72 in, white fabric

Pattern pieces
Using a rotary cutter, cut patchwork fabrics across the width into strips 1⅝ in wide, then into 1⅝ in squares. Assuming that you are going to use the same number of fabrics and to repeat fabrics in the same order as in the original quilt, cut squares as follows:

    Fabric 2 (middle): 72
    Fabric 3: 372
    Fabric 4: 28
    Fabric 5: 76
    Fabric 6 (white): 340
    Fabric 7: 44
    Fabric 8: 188
    Fabric 9: 52
    Fabric 10: 56
    Fabric 11: 160
    Fabric 12: 254
    Fabric 13: 208
    Fabric 14: 292
    Fabric 15: 192
    Fabric 16: 166
    Fabric 17: 168
    Fabric 18: 116
    Fabric 19: 124
    Fabric 20: 188
    Fabric 21: 144
    Fabric 22: 152
    Fabric 23: 160, 80
    Fabric 24: 82

PIECING

1 The patches are pieced together in diagonal rows, and because so many fabrics are used, you must organize your work before starting to join the patches. It helps to have an enlarged photocopy made of the assembly diagram, so you can cross off rows as they are joined. If you are using fewer or more fabrics than those specified here, or changing the order in which fabrics are repeated, make an assembly diagram before starting.

2 Put your patches in bags, one for each fabric, with the fabric number marked on the bag.

3 The patchwork is stitched together in diagonal rows, from one corner across to the opposite corner.

  If you are hand sewing, complete each row before moving on to the next, then go to step 6. However, if you are machine stitching, you can either work in complete rows, or you can follow the method shown from step 4.

4 For speed sewing, work from the bottom row of the quilt upward. First join the two patches (one white, one of fabric 12) at the bottom left-hand corner. Without cutting the thread, join the next two patches (one white, one fabric 24), the next (white, fabric 16), then the next two (white, 23). Join 40 more pairs of white and dark-blue (23) patches, and then the right-hand border patches. You will now have a long string of patches, joined in pairs.

5 Starting at one end of the string, cut away the first pair of patches (these two make the first complete corner row), and set them aside. Join a fabric 23 (dark-blue) patch to the next pair, a fabric 17 patch to the next, a white patch to the next, and then a fabric 20 patch to the next 40 pairs, finishing with the border rows. Leave each pair of patches on the first string until you are ready to add the next patch; this helps you keep the rows in the correct order.

6 Rows can be joined as they are completed, or when all rows are completed. Take care to match seamlines when joining rows. Join the patchwork into two halves, then join down the middle to complete the top.

7 Carefully press the patchwork. Turn under a ¼ in seam allowance on each raw edge; press and baste. Make the corners as neat as possible.

8 The patchwork is appliquéd to the border strips. Take the shorter, wider strips and pin and baste them to the top and bottom of the patchwork. In each case, lay the patchwork over the border strip, and make sure that there are 3⅛ in of border fabric extending beyond the corners of the patchwork squares.
Lay the work on a flat surface, and pin from the middle outward to each corner; do not stretch the fabric. Fold the seam allowance under at each end of the border strips.

9 Take the remaining border strips, and lay the sides over these strips in the same manner, this time leaving 1 in of border fabric extending beyond the corners of the patchwork

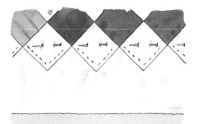

squares. The folded ends of the top and bottom border strips should lie over the raw edges of the side strips.
Pin and baste the border strips carefully in position.

10 Using very small, neat blind stitches, taken through the pressed edges of the patchwork squares and down through the border strips, attach the patchwork to the border strips. Top stitch or blind stitch the border pieces together.

11 When the border has been joined to the patchwork, cut away any spare border fabric from behind the patchwork, leaving just a ¼ in seam allowance.

12 To complete the quilt back, join the two fabric pieces together along the long edge,

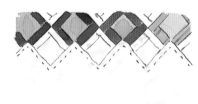

and press the seam allowance to one side.

13 Assemble the top, batting and backing (see page 13).

FINISHING
14 The quilting is very simple, just horizontal and vertical lines running through each patchwork square. Quilting lines should not extend beyond the patchwork at

the sides, and should stop 1 in clear of the raw edges at the top and bottom of the quilt.

15 Turn under a ¼ in seam allowance all around the border and take the folded edge to the back of the quilt, mitring the corners. Pin, baste and then stitch.

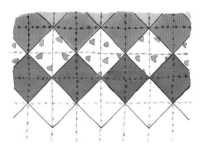

RIGHT This detail shows the clever mingling of plain and patterned fabrics in this quilt.

Templates

To save space the templates on the following pages overlap. They will need to be enlarged, by the amount specified, on a photocopier. After enlarging the template, trace it out and stick the paper to a sturdy material such as durable cardboard. If you are going to hand-sew your quilt you do not need to add a seam allowance to the templates, but if machine-sewing, allow 6mm/1/4 in seam around the outline of the template. For more information, see page 11, How to Begin. Templates drawn with solid lines are for patchwork, those drawn with dotted lines are for quilting. For further information on quilting, see page 13.

KEY

Hex	Hexagon Star	*page 124*
A.S.	Adirondack Star	*page 124, 126*
C.B.*	Crazy Bear	*page 122*
D.B.	Durham Basket	*page 123, 126*
O.W.	Ocean Waves	*page 124, 126*
L.of L.	Lady of the Lake	*page 124*
S. in S.	Sun in Splendour	*page 121, 123, 125, 126*
T. in a P.	Toad in a Puddle	*page 122*
B. C.	Bordered Chain	*page 121*
S.H.	Schoolhouse	*page 124*
R.C.	Roman Cross	*page 123*
C. of Th.	Crown of Thorns	*page 124, 125*

* For templates which cross the middle of the book first trace the left-hand page, including dotted lines, then line up your tracing with the dotted line of the pattern on the right-hand page to complete the template.

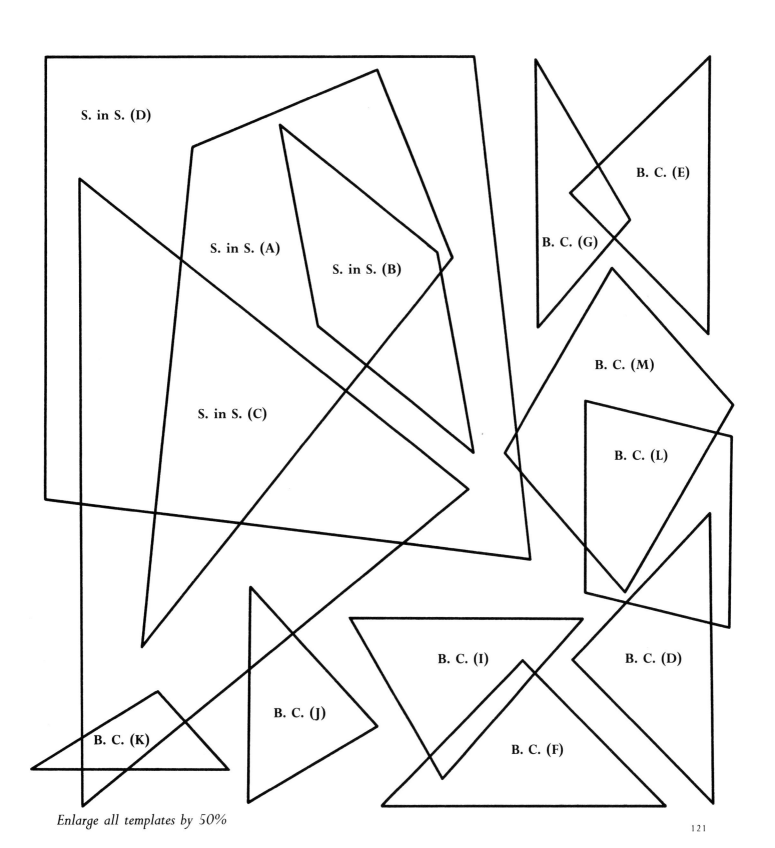

S. in S. (D)

S. in S. (A)

S. in S. (B)

S. in S. (C)

B. C. (E)

B. C. (G)

B. C. (M)

B. C. (L)

B. C. (I)

B. C. (D)

B. C. (J)

B. C. (K)

B. C. (F)

Enlarge all templates by 50%

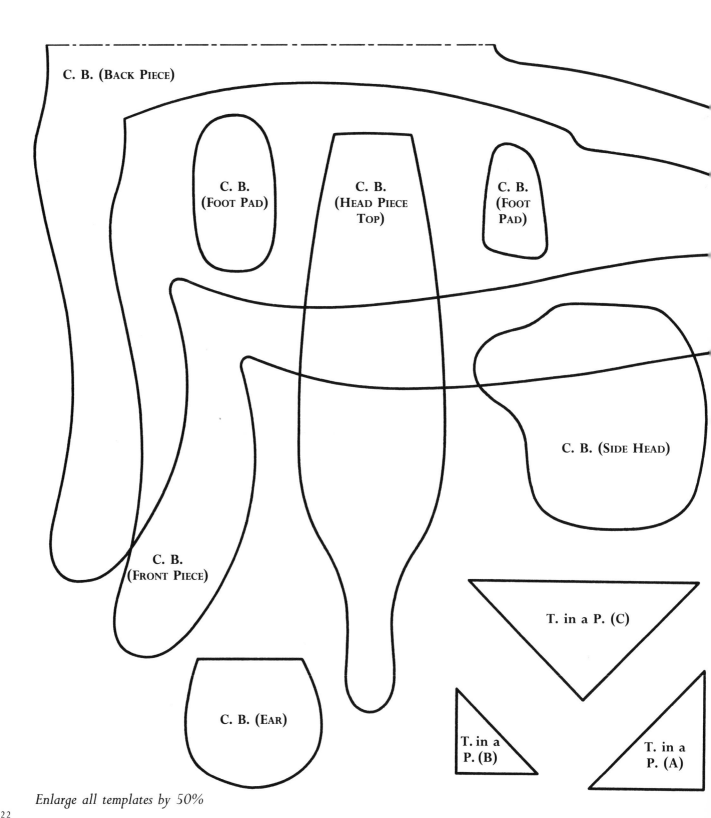

C. B. (Back Piece)

C. B. (Foot Pad)

C. B. (Head Piece Top)

C. B. (Foot Pad)

C. B. (Side Head)

C. B. (Front Piece)

C. B. (Ear)

T. in a P. (C)

T. in a P. (B)

T. in a P. (A)

Enlarge all templates by 50%

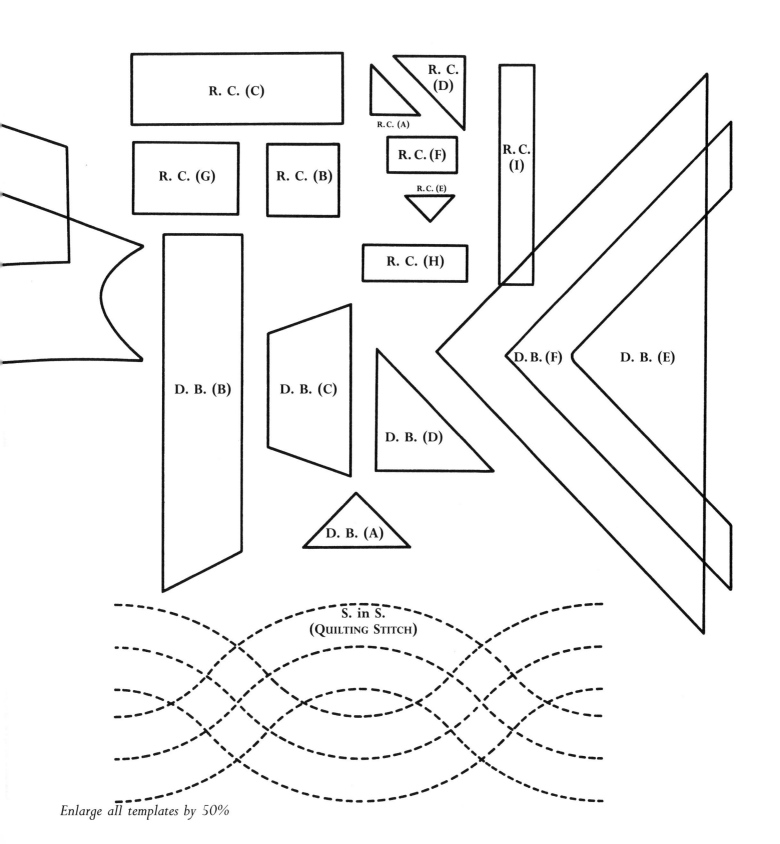

R. C. (C)

R. C. (D)

R.C. (A)

R. C. (F)

R. C. (G)

R. C. (B)

R.C. (E)

R. C. (H)

R.C. (I)

D. B. (B)

D. B. (C)

D. B. (D)

D.B. (F)

D. B. (E)

D. B. (A)

S. in S.
(QUILTING STITCH)

Enlarge all templates by 50%

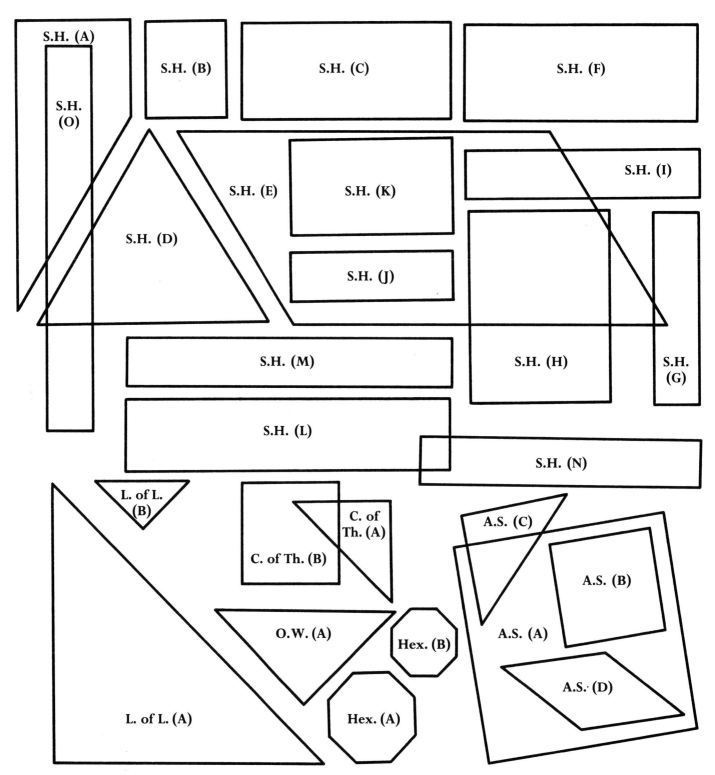

Enlarge all templates by 50%

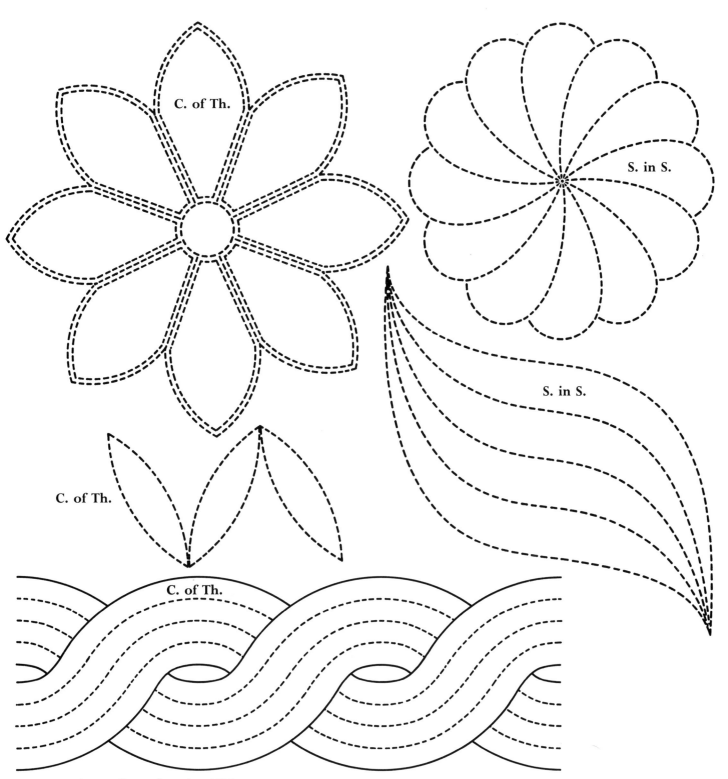

C. of Th.

S. in S.

S. in S.

C. of Th.

C. of Th.

Enlarge all templates by 40%

Enlarge all templates by 40% apart from Durham Basket template which is actual size.

Index

Acknowledgments

The author and publishers would like to thank Jane Cumberbatch for her help in finding the quilts featured, and the following people who loaned them: Tobias & the Angel, 68 White Hart Lane, London SW13; Marilyn Garrow, 6 The Broadway, London SW13; Tricia Jameson Design, 4 Sydney Place, London SW7; Judy Greenwood Antiques, 657 Fulham Road, London SW6; and Susan Jenkins, Museum Quilts Gallery, 3rd Floor, 254-258 Goswell Road, London EC1.